TABL

MW01487589

━━━━━━━━━●━○━●●━━━

Unless otherwise indicated, all Scripture quotations are taken from the King James Version of the Bible.

The Uncommon Woman · ISBN 1-56394-214-3/B-146

Copyright © 2010 by *MIKE MURDOCK*

Publisher/Editor: Deborah Murdock Johnson

Published by The Wisdom Center · 4051 Denton Hwy. · Ft. Worth, Texas 76117

1-817-759-BOOK · 1-817-759-2665 · 1-817-759-0300

You Will Love Our Website..! WisdomOnline.com

Printed in the United States of America. All rights reserved under International Copyright Law. Contents and/or cover may not be reproduced in whole or in part in any form without the express written consent of the publisher.

Passion Is
Simply What
You Are Unwilling
To Live Without.

-MIKE MURDOCK

Copyright © 2010 by Mike Murdock • Wisdom International
The Wisdom Center • 4051 Denton Hwy. • Ft. Worth, TX 76117

WHY I WROTE THIS BOOK

Passion Is Power.

You Will Only Have Significant Success With Something That Is An Obsession. An Obsession is when something consumes your *thoughts* and *time*. *Passion Is Simply What You Are Unwilling To Live Without.*

You Will Only Be Remembered In Life For Your Obsession.

▶ Florence Nightingale is remembered as the Pioneer of Modern *Nursing.*

▶ Rosa Parks...The Mother of the Modern-Day *Civil Rights Movement.*

▶ Mother Teresa...*Missionaries of Charity* in Calcutta, India.

▶ Madame Curie...a Pioneer of *Radioactivity,* the first person ever to win two *Nobel Prizes.*

You are NOT an ordinary woman. God made you the *EXTRAORDINARY Woman.*

You are The Uncommon Woman!

That is why I wrote this book.

Mike Murdock

You Will Only Be
    Remembered In Life
For Two Things:
    The Problems You Solve
or The Ones You Create.

-MIKE MURDOCK

Copyright © 2010 by Mike Murdock • Wisdom International
The Wisdom Center • 4051 Denton Hwy. • Ft. Worth, TX 76117

⚘ 1 ⚘

THE UNCOMMON WOMAN WILL ALWAYS FOCUS HER ENERGY TOWARD HER FUTURE

━━━━━━⮞❖⮜━━━━━━

Become A "Tomorrow Thinker."

Make your *Future* so *significant* that *Yesterday* disappears.

Ruth created a *Future* different from her *Past.*

Who was Ruth? Ruth was a Moabite girl raised in heathenism. To grasp the culture in which Ruth was reared, Moab was the son of incest between Lot and his daughter.

Ruth married Boaz who, according to one writer, had come through the loins of a temple prostitute by the name of Rahab. God put them together...and *ushered* in the lineage of Jesus Christ. (See Ruth 4:13-22.)

Ruth and Boaz produced Obed. Obed produced Jesse. Jesse produced David. David ushered in the lineage of Jesus Christ.

Ruth was the *great-grandmother* of *David,* the greatest warrior Israel has ever known. She was the *great-great-grandmother* of Solomon, one of the wisest men who ever lived on earth.

Through Ruth and Boaz came the precious Son of

the living God, Jesus of Nazareth.

God Never Consults Your Past To Decide Your Future. Satan may remind you of Yesterday's mistakes. Do not listen to him.

Your Past is over.

▶ *Act* like it.
▶ *Talk* like it.
▶ *Live* like it.

The Uncommon Woman Will Always Focus Her Energy Toward Her Future.

RECOMMENDED INVESTMENTS:
Dream Seeds (Book/B-11/106 pg)
Seeds of Wisdom on Dreams & Goals (Book/B-13/32 pg)
Secrets of The Journey, Vol. 7 (Book/B-103/32 pg)
You Will Love Our Website..! WisdomOnline.com

≈ 2 ≈

THE UNCOMMON WOMAN IS WILLING TO GO WHERE SHE HAS NEVER BEEN BEFORE

Geography Makes A Difference.

It is possible you will need to change locations to *unlock* the full potential of your success.

Pineapples grow well in Hawaii. However, they barely survive in Alaska. Any Seed will grow in the *appropriate* climate. "Also I heard the voice of the Lord, saying, Whom shall I send, and who will go for us? Then said I, Here am I; send me," (Isaiah 6:8).

You Are A Seed. Everything you have is a Seed... your Business and Products are like Seeds.

Your Future Is A Harvest Produced By The Seed You Are Willing To Sow.

Success Requires People. You will never succeed without networking with people of *varied* interests.

They may not be easily accessible. You may have to leave the comforts of your home to achieve *extraordinary* success.

Jesus was in constant movement, changing locations, *arising, departing* and *going* to new places. He sought to be around people of *varied* backgrounds.

"When He was come down from the mountain, great multitudes followed Him," (Matthew 8:1). "And when Jesus was entered into Capernaum, there came unto Him a centurion, beseeching Him," (Matthew 8:5). "And when Jesus was come into Peter's house, He saw his wife's mother laid, and sick of a fever," (Matthew 8:14).

Some people will not come where you are. You may have to search for them in their home, town or *their own* environment.

Jesus told His disciples to go to the Upper Room... *a different place.* They were to tarry there until they received the experience of The Holy Spirit. (See Luke 24:49.)

He gave this instruction to 500 of His followers. Even after they had observed His resurrection and His miracle life, only 120 out of the 500 actually *followed* and *obeyed* His instruction. (See Acts 1:15.)

Abraham, the Patriarch of the Israelites, had to make geographical changes before his success was birthed. (See Genesis 12:1-2.)

Joseph found his incredible success in another country...Egypt. (See Genesis 41:39-44.)

The Uncommon Woman Is Willing To Go Where She Has Never Been Before.

RECOMMENDED INVESTMENTS:
7 Kinds of People Who Always Fail (CD/WCPL-06)
7 Relationship Secrets of Abraham (CD/WCPL-50)
You Will Love Our Website..! WisdomOnline.com

❧ **3** ❧

THE UNCOMMON WOMAN CREATES AN ENVIRONMENT OF ORDER AND MOTIVATION

Order Creates Comfort.

Take a small step toward order each day.

Order is placing an item where it belongs.

Order is placing clothing and shoes in the *appropriate* place in your closet. Every *tiny* act of your life will increase *order* or *disorder* around you.

Order Is Simply The Accurate Arrangement of Things.

The purpose of order is to *increase productivity* and *create comfort.* This is done so that when you walk into an orderly room, you have a *desire* to stay. Things just feel *"right."* You feel *clean, energized* and *happy.*

When you walk *into* a room dominated by clutter and disorder, an *unexplainable* agitation begins. Perhaps you cannot identify or understand, but you know it is there.

You were *created* for order...anything that slows you down emotionally or mentally will become a *distraction* and cause you to *lose focus.*

When you *increase* order, you will increase your

productivity. Filing cabinets, trays on the desk and special places for folders make it easier to get your job done on time.

Have you ever shuffled paper after paper while searching for a bill? Of course you have! By the time you finally locate the bill, you have become agitated and angry.

Disorder influences your *attitude* more than you could ever imagine. Everything you do affects the level of order in your life.

Think for a moment. When you get up from the breakfast table you will either *leave* your plate on the table, or you will *take* it to the sink. The decision you make will either *increase* or *decrease* the order around you. (Leaving it on the table increases your workload and creates disorder. Taking it to the sink *immediately* promotes order.)

This happened to me last night. I took off my suit coat and laid it over the chair. I did not really feel like taking it to the closet to hang it up. However, realizing that I was going to have to hang it up *eventually,* I walked over to the closet and hung up my coat. I *immediately* increased order around me. I like the feeling order creates.

▶ *Every Moment, You Are Increasing Order or Creating Disorder In Your Life.*

▶ *Small Actions Will Eventually Produce Desired Results.*

▶ *Every Person Around You Is Increasing Order or Disorder.*

Some people have an *attitude* of disorder. They almost seem unhappy unless everything is in disarray. Others refuse to work in such an environment...*their* productivity *requires* organization.

Just 20 minutes a day to restore order can make a major difference in your surroundings. *Little* hinges swing *big* doors. You can get anywhere you want to go if you are willing to take *enough* small steps.

The Uncommon Woman Creates An Environment of Order And Motivation.

RECOMMENDED INVESTMENT:
12 Ingredients of A Perfect Day, Vols. 1-2 (2 CDs/WCPL-56)
You Will Love Our Website..! WisdomOnline.com

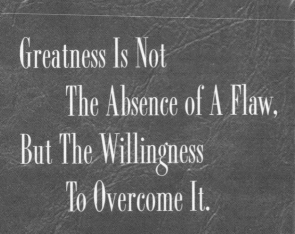

Greatness Is Not
        The Absence of A Flaw,
But The Willingness
        To Overcome It.

-MIKE MURDOCK

Copyright © 2010 by Mike Murdock • Wisdom International
The Wisdom Center • 4051 Denton Hwy. • Ft. Worth, TX 76117

≋ 4 ≋

THE UNCOMMON WOMAN CORRECTLY ASSESSES HER EMOTIONS TO CREATE A DESIRED FUTURE

—————⟫⟩•◊•⟨⟪—————

Your Life Is Worth Every Investment.

The first thing I do every morning is to listen to the Scriptures on my iPod.

I purchase candles of the fragrance I enjoy most, with the strongest scent that last the longest. Placing candles around my room helps to provide an *incredible* atmosphere of reflection and warmth.

I need that.

My *Heart* and my *Mind* require it.

A few days ago, I spent over $100 on several CDs. Yet, when I purchased them, I was not just purchasing some music on compact discs. *I was creating the atmosphere that benefits me.*

Recreate this scenario for yourself.

After listening to the Bible on my iPod this morning, I turned on the CD player. These 6 CDs contained the sounds of *birds,* a sparkling flowing *fountain* and *peaceful* music. Within seconds, I felt as though I was under the trees, tasting the richness of God's nature around me. Yet, I was in my bedroom! I did not have to spend $2,000 to take a vacation to Honolulu. I simply needed an *investment* in my atmosphere.

Each atmosphere produces a different emotion. An interior decorator or the suggestions of a friend can help you *discover* and *design* the atmosphere you prefer to work in, or just relax.

Do Not Wait On Others To Initiate Changes In Your Environment. Make any investment necessary to create the environment that *inspires* you toward excellence and the improvement of your life.

Your Investment In Interior Decorating Can Make A Huge Difference In Your Productivity. A new rug, a picture on the wall or a vase with a rose can increase the warmth of your *environment.*

Invest And Experiment To Discover What You Really Need Around You. It is exciting to explore variations in your environment.

Your Atmosphere Can Often Determine Your Productivity. Many businesses have discovered an increase in unity and employee morale when music is played quietly throughout their offices.

What You See Affects The Decisions You Make. It does not cost a fortune to create a *favorable* atmosphere. Just *think...look* and *ask* questions. Explore and Experiment.

Invest Whatever Is Necessary To Create The Atmosphere You Want To Surround You.

The Uncommon Woman Correctly Assesses Her Emotions To Create A Desired Future.

❧ 5 ❧

THE UNCOMMON WOMAN IS NOT AFRAID TO FAIL EN ROUTE TO SUCCESS

"No" Simply Means "Ask Again."
All Men Fall, The Great Ones Get Back Up.

Stay persistent. "And let us not be weary in well doing: for in due season we shall reap, if we faint not," (Galatians 6:9).

Rejection is not fatal. It is merely someone's opinion. Stop for a moment. Review your experiences. Maybe you encountered rejection when you were a child. Nevertheless, you have made it this far, which proves you are a survivor!

Jesus experienced more rejection than any human being who ever lived on the earth. He was born in a stable...an *outcast* in society.

Even today, the hosts of television talk shows belittle and ridicule both He and His followers. He was rejected by His own people. "He came unto His own, and His own received Him not," (John 1:11).

When Judas betrayed Him, did He allow Himself to become demoralized? Did He quit? No.

Jesus knew that He did not have to close every sale to become a success. *Those He went to discerned His value.* "But as many as received Him, to them gave

He power to become the sons of God, even to them that believe on His name," (John 1:12).

Jesus knew His *worth* and what He had to *offer to others*. Jesus knew His critics would die...but His *plan* was eternal. He was willing to experience a *Season* of Pain...to create an *Eternity* of Gain. (See Hebrews 12:2.)

Your *Goals* and *Dreams* will last longer than any rejection you may experience. Move beyond your *scars*. Not everyone will *celebrate* or welcome your Future.

But *someone* needs what you have to offer. Your *contribution* is an absolute *necessity* for their success.

Discern it.

The religious sect, called Sadducees, rejected Jesus, as did the Pharisees. The religious leaders despised The Christ. Those who *should* have recognized His worth, instead wanted to *destroy* Him. (See Matthew 26:3-4.)

Jesus risked rejection to become The Golden Link between man and God. (See Hebrews 12:2.)

Most great sales representatives know that 14 out of 15 people will say *"no"* to their sales pitch. They say this merely inspires them to hurry and make their presentations to as many as possible, to reach that one who *will* accept.

Jesus taught His disciples how to handle rejection. "And whosoever shall not receive you, nor hear your words, when ye depart out of that house or city, shake off the dust of your feet," (Matthew 10:14).

So, get up off your recliner.

Make that telephone call.

Write that letter.

Eventually you will succeed.

The Uncommon Woman Is Not Afraid To Fail En Route To Success.

6

THE UNCOMMON WOMAN IS DIRECT AND DECISIVE

Develop Decisiveness.

Have you ever noticed the *hesitation* in drivers at a 4-way stop? I have seen people sit for 30 seconds at a 4-way stop waiting for everyone else to make the first move!

I have sat at restaurants with people who could not decide in 20 minutes what food they wanted to eat! Some have even asked the waitress what she thought they should eat!

Few people are decisive.

Think about what you want.

Invest the Seed of Time to become decisive.

Contemplate the *value* of your decisions.

Meditate upon the *results* of your decisions.

Questions Concerning Your Future

▶ *What Do You Want To Be Happening In Your Life 10 Years From Today?*

▶ *What Are The Ideal Circumstances For Your Retirement?*

▶ *What Do You Dream of Becoming?*

▶ *Do You Have A Personal List of Goals And*

Dreams?
► *Have You Taken Time To Write The Details of Your Goals?*

Several years ago, a brilliant young lady suggested that I take a tape recorder, walk into each room of my home and describe clearly what I wished that room to look like. Something wonderful happened! I described exactly how many pens and pencils I wanted in the different areas. I recall even going into such detail as to describe the kind of paper I wanted beside my telephone.

I found the process to be *elaborate, energizing* and *exciting.* Few people invest the time to discover what motivates them.

Something interesting happened in my personal meditation time some weeks ago. I had become concerned by how *frequently* my interests seemed to change.

For example, the colors my decorator selected for my home were exciting and pleasing to me. I felt I would *never* want to change my mind about them for years to come. However, a few weeks later, I discovered another combination of colors that excited me even *more.*

Obviously, I did not feel comfortable about suddenly altering everything that had just been changed in my home. Nor, did I really have the finances to do so.

Another example was when I purchased a car. I loved it...*for about 3 weeks!* Then, I became bored and wanted a *change.*

I felt impressed of The Holy Spirit to write down a list of things that had never changed inside me over many years. It was quite an interesting list of things. This helped to really put my mind at ease that there was more *stability* within me than I realized.

Many things within me have never changed whatsoever, such as my love for *information,* my desire to collect *books* or the excitement that comes along with receiving a rare, new *coin* from a beloved friend.

Another thing that has remained constant is my *continual* need to recreate my environment. Regardless of how beautiful my bedroom or kitchen is...within 12 months or so, I lose interest and want to redecorate. This has been consistent.

Some things will never change about you.

What are they? Put this book down for about 15 minutes. Take a sheet of paper, and as quickly and thoroughly as possible, begin to document the things about yourself that have been fairly *consistent* over the years. Go ahead. *Do it now.*

After you have done this, you will have a more accurate and specific photograph of certain things that you want to experience in your daily life. You will also have an awareness of the *quality* of life you need.

Some years ago, I asked a consultant to come into my offices for several days. He was to discuss any complaints or ideas with each of my staff. Then I wanted him to compile a report, *unbiased* and *unprejudiced,* as to what he had observed about our ministry organization.

He interrogated me for hours. He would take long walks and rides with me in the car. Even when I was in crusades, we would talk by telephone. His *constant questioning* served to remarkably *sharpen* my focus. I have never forgotten this experience.

The consultant was relentless in collecting data about my personal needs, desires and appetites concerning life. *Riveting questions were hurled at me continually.*

Listed below are 8 questions you can use in this marvelous exercise.

It will change your life.

1.   What Were The Happiest Moments of Your Lifetime?

2.   What Are The 3 Biggest Problems You Think About The Most During Every Day?

3.   Who Are The People You Find Stressful To Be Around?

4.   Who Are The People In Whose Presence You Are The Most Relaxed?

5.   How Do You Want Others To Remember You?

6.   What Do You Consider The Most Important Task You Do *Daily...Weekly...Monthly?*

7.   If You Had To Eliminate 50 Percent of Your Entire Workload, What Would You Change?

8.   If You Were To Have A Sudden Health Crisis, or Some Other Medical Emergency, What Would You Change First About Your Daily Lifestyle?

Slowly but surely, a remarkable *understanding* of what you *really* want out of life will be developed. Ask one or two of your closest friends who are skilled at analyzing your personal situation to interrogate you for helpful information.

Let these friends extract information from you until you have a complete *photograph* of the invisible Future you desire to create and bring into reality.

Something is *driving* you...*pushing* you toward your Future. What is the invisible Dream you are subconsciously trying to birth within yourself?

Decisiveness Is Magnetic. Decisiveness is the catalyst that helps create the aura that surrounds *extraordinary* and *unforgettable* people.

These people know *exactly* what they want.

When you are sitting in a restaurant sometime, conduct this test. Carefully observe the entry of customers. Notice those who *saunter* in as if they are not quite certain they have chosen the right restaurant. They slowly walk to their seats wondering if they should even stay. Perhaps they wonder if they should select a different table.

Then, observe carefully those who stride in confidently and with a *firm, clear* voice, express to the hostess of the restaurant, "Good evening! We need a table for 4—by the window, if possible!" Notice how the hostess responds *quickly,* with enthusiasm to communicate this request to the other workers.

When ordering your own meal at a restaurant, speak up. Speak firmly. Do not mumble.

Someone has said, "If you will raise your voice 10 percent and walk 20 percent faster, you will generate remarkable new energy. This activity will compel others to respond *favorably* to you and raise the level of self-confidence in every single person around you."

James said it this way, "But let him ask in faith, nothing wavering. For he that wavereth is like a wave of the sea driven with the wind and tossed. For let not that man think that he shall receive any thing of the Lord. A double minded man is unstable in all his ways," (James 1:6-8).

What happens when you are *indecisive* about an issue? There is a *reason* for your uncertainty. It may be lack of *sufficient* information or absence of *accurate* information. When this happens, simply declare with great decisiveness, "I will wait 90 days until I receive *additional* information."

This decisive attitude will help you to retain your climate of confidence and decisiveness.

Make Decisions With Clarity.

Notice how Ruth stated quite clearly, "Whither thou goest, I will go; and where thou lodgest, I will lodge," (Ruth 1:16).

Ruth knew what she wanted and boldly communicated this wish to Naomi.

The Uncommon Woman Is Direct And Decisive.

RECOMMENDED INVESTMENTS:
The Proverbs 31 Woman (Book/B-49/70 pg)
The Making of A Champion (Book/B-59/128 pg)
The Mentor's Manna On Achievement (Book/B-79/32 pg)
You Will Love Our Website..! WisdomOnline.com

❧ 7 ❧

THE UNCOMMON WOMAN SETS GOALS AND UPDATES THEM CONTINUOUSLY

Decide What You Really Want.

In 1952, a prominent university discovered that only 3 out of 100 graduates had written down a clear list of goals.

Ten years later, their follow-up study showed that 3 percent of the graduating class had accomplished more financially than the remaining 97 percent of the class combined.

You Will Never Leave Where You Are Until You Decide Where You Would Rather Be.

The 3 percent that *accomplished* their goals were the same graduates who had *written* down their goals. "Write the vision, and make it plain upon tables, that he may run that readeth it," (Habakkuk 2:2).

When you decide exactly *'What'* you want, the *'How to do it'* will emerge.

When Your Heart Decides The Destination, Your Mind Will Design The Map To Reach It.

Jesus knew both His *Purpose* and *Mission.* "For the Son of man is come to seek and to save that which was lost," (Luke 19:10).

Jesus knew the *product* He had to offer. "The thief cometh not, but for to steal, and to kill, and to destroy: I am come that they might have life, and that they might have it more abundantly," (John 10:10).

Jesus had a sense of *Destiny,* knowing where He wanted to go. Jesus knew where He was needed. (Read John 4:3.) "For which of you, intending to build a tower, sitteth not down first, and counteth the cost, whether he have sufficient to finish it?" (Luke 14:28).

4 Steps Toward Accomplishing Goals

Gather 4 sheets of paper.

1.   **On the first page write, "My Lifetime Dreams and Goals."** List in detail what you would like to *Become, Do* or *Have* during your Lifetime.

2.   **On the second page write, "My 12 Month Goals."** List everything you plan to accomplish within the next 12 months.

3.   **On the third page write, "My 30 Day Goals."** List in detail the things you would like to accomplish during the next 30 days.

4.   **On the fourth page write, "My Daily Routine."** Write the 6 most important rituals you plan to perform daily.

The Secret of Your Future Is Hidden In Your Daily Routine.

As you set your goals keep in mind they will *change* throughout your lifetime. Some day, you will look back at this very moment and be amazed at the goals you presently have.

Things that were so vital to you at age 20 will *change* and seem *unimportant* when you reach 30 years of age.

At the beginning of my ministry, I wanted very much to minister in many different states and cities. The very idea of travel thrilled me.

Times have changed.

Today, staying at home excites me. Knowing my books are read in many parts of the world is much more satisfying to me than traveling the globe.

The greatest goal of my life today is staying in my Secret Place of prayer and writing what The Holy Spirit teaches me through His Word and my daily experiences.

The Uncommon Woman Sets Goals And Updates Them Continuously.

RECOMMENDED INVESTMENTS:
Dream Seeds (Book/B-11/106 pg)
Seeds of Wisdom on Dreams & Goals (Book/B-13/32 pg)
Secrets of The Journey, Vol. 7 (Book/B-103/32 pg)
You Will Love Our Website..! WisdomOnline.com

Your Future
Is Decided
By What You
Are Willing To Change.

-MIKE MURDOCK

Copyright © 2010 by Mike Murdock • Wisdom International
The Wisdom Center • 4051 Denton Hwy. • Ft. Worth, TX 76117

∾ 8 ∾

THE UNCOMMON WOMAN ANTICIPATES CHANGES IN HER GOALS AND DREAMS

Dreams Are Given To Inspire.

Allow *unexciting* dreams to die. When you assess and evaluate your goals, *unnecessary* activities will be revealed.

6 Strategies For The Uncommon Woman Concerning Dreams And Goals

1.   Invest One Hour In Writing Down Goals That Really Matter To You Today. Keep these strategies confidential. "Write the vision, and make it plain upon tables, that he may run that readeth it," (Habakkuk 2:2).

2.   Allow The Unexciting Dreams of Yesterday To Die. Stop pursuing anything that does not have the ability to excite you. Do not feel obligated to keep trying to obtain expired goals...if you have entered a different season. (See Isaiah 43:18-19.)

3.   Do Not Expect Others To Understand Your Dreams And Goals. Permit them their individuality, also. They have every right to choose the things they love. Refuse to be intimidated when acquaintances try to persuade you to go in a different direction.

4. Never Make Permanent Decisions Because of Temporary Feelings. One young lady was so excited about a new friend that she dropped the lease on her own apartment and moved into the residence of her new friend. Within a week, she realized her mistake!

5. Avoid Intimate Relationships With Those Who Do Not Respect Your Dreams. You will have to sever ties with wrong people. They do not always leave your life *voluntarily*. Life is too short to permit "discouragers" to live in close proximity to you. "And have no fellowship with the unfruitful works of darkness, but rather reprove them," (Ephesians 5:11).

6. Anticipate Changes In Your Goals. Your present feelings and opinions are not permanent. New experiences and different types of relationships are in your Future. Remain conscious of this principle.

The Uncommon Woman Anticipates Changes In Her Goals And Dreams.

RECOMMENDED INVESTMENT:
Seeds of Wisdom on Dreams & Goals (Book/B-13/32 pg)
You Will Love Our Website..! WisdomOnline.com

9

THE UNCOMMON WOMAN IS CONFIDENT OF HER WORTH

Emotions Dictate The World.
"The righteous are bold as a lion," (Proverbs 28:1).
Boldness Decides Rulership.
An angered world leader attacks another country.
Upset airline employees man a picket line at the airport.

A mother whose child is killed by a drunk driver launches a national campaign.

Thousands are rallying to stop the abortion of millions of babies.

Feelings Really Do Matter In Life.

Feelings are *contagious.* When a salesman is excited over his product, the customer *feels* that enthusiasm, and is *influenced* by that display of excitement.

Jesus was not afraid to express Himself. When He was infuriated, *others* knew it. "And the Jews' passover was at hand, and Jesus went up to Jerusalem, And found in the temple those that sold oxen and sheep and doves, and the changers of money sitting: And when He had made a scourge of small cords, He drove them all out of the temple, and the sheep, and the oxen; and poured out the changers' money, and overthrew the tables," (John 2:13-15).

He was deeply moved with compassion when He saw multitudes wandering aimlessly without direction. "But when He saw the multitudes, He was moved with compassion on them, because they fainted, and were scattered abroad, as sheep having no shepherd," (Matthew 9:36).

The Bible even records that Jesus wept *openly* over the needs of humanity. "And when He was come near, He beheld the city, and wept over it," (Luke 19:41).

Are you bold in expressing your opinions?

I am not speaking about an uncontrollable temper, nor am I referring to someone who has an emotional breakdown every time a problem occurs.

Rather, I am reminding you that Jesus did not bottle up His emotions. He was not a robot.

He was *enthusiastic* when He saw a display of *faith.* He *wept* when He saw *unbelief.*

Peter, His disciple, was affected by those expressions of emotions. The Apostle Paul was set on fire by these reactions. These two men changed the course of history.

Be bold, yet correct when expressing your opinions in the proper manner. You will be an influence for good if you are *focused* upon the things that really matter.

You will always be drawn to expressive people. Do not be a spectator just viewing life. Get in the arena. Thousands scream with excitement at rock concerts, football games and World-Championship boxing matches.

Do not be afraid to display your true feelings...at

the appropriate time and place.

Significant leaders build their *daily agenda* around their Assignment. Their schedule and their plans are totally focused upon the *completion* of their Assignment. Their library is filled with books related to their Assignment. Leaders become best friends with those who celebrate (rather than *tolerate*) their Assignment.

When you hear the name, Thomas Edison...you think *inventions.*

When you hear the name, Oral Roberts...you think *healing.*

When you hear the name, Henry Ford...you think *automobile.*

When you hear the name, Michael Jordan...you think *basketball.*

You Will Only Be Remembered For Your Obsession. It may be a *good* obsession or an *evil* obsession. Whether you are Billy Graham or Adolph Hitler...you will be remembered for what consumes your *mind* and your *time.*

Ruth did not pursue the normal path of dating others. She built her lifestyle around the survival of her mother-in-law Naomi. She *never* considered another option.

Your obsession may be your personal business. Or you may be obsessed with the spiritual life of your children.

You will succeed with anything that has the ability to capture your *total focus.*

Joshua called it, "not looking to the right or to the left." Others call it being *"single-minded."* James said, "A double minded man is unstable in all his ways," (James 1:8).

Ruth refused to consider any alternatives to her Assignment. She would not go back to her in-laws or return to the village of her youth. Ruth had developed total focus on her Assignment.

The Only Reason Men Fail Is Broken Focus. If you fail in life, it will be because something was suggested to you as an *alternative* option to what God told you to do with your life.

Consider Moses. The Bible says, "By faith Moses, when he was come to years, refused to be called the son of Pharaoh's daughter; Choosing rather to suffer affliction with the people of God, than to enjoy the pleasures of sin for a season; Esteeming the reproach of Christ greater riches than the treasures in Egypt: for he had respect unto the recompence of the reward," (Hebrews 11:24-26).

The Uncommon Woman will pursue her Future with *confidence* that she has what it takes to succeed in life.

The Uncommon Woman Is Confident of Her Worth.

RECOMMENDED INVESTMENTS:
The Leadership Secrets of Jesus (Book/B-91/196 pg)
Secrets of The Richest Man Who Ever Lived (Book/B-99/179 pg)
You Will Love Our Website..! WisdomOnline.com

❧ 10 ❧

THE UNCOMMON WOMAN MOTIVATES HERSELF WHEN OTHERS ARE UNCARING

────⟫•◉•⟪────

There Is No "Plan B" For Your Life.

There is only one plan...The Master Plan of the Creator Who made you.

Consider nothing else as an option.

This made Ruth The Uncommon Woman.

As Naomi walked with her two daughters-in-law, Orpah and Ruth, she turned and said, "Go, return each to her mother's house: the Lord deal kindly with you, as ye have dealt with the dead, and with me. The Lord grant you that ye may find rest, each of you in the house of her husband. Then she kissed them; and they lifted up their voice, and wept," (Ruth 1:8-9).

Naomi kissed both her daughters-in-law as they wept. Both said, "We will return with thee unto thy people."

However Naomi instructed, "Turn again, my daughters: why will ye go with me? are there yet any more sons in my womb, that they may be your husbands? Turn again, my daughters, go your way; for I am too old to have an husband. If I should say, I have hope, if I should have an husband also to night, and should also bear sons," (Ruth 1:11-12).

They lifted up their voice. They wept again.

Orpah left. Yet, Ruth *cleaved* unto her. Naomi rebuked Ruth, "Behold, thy sister in law is gone back unto her people, and unto her gods: return thou after thy sister in law," (Ruth 1:15).

Ruth was *tenacious...bold* and *focused*. Yes, her husband and father-in-law were both dead. Her sister-in-law had returned to her family. Her mother-in-law instructed her to return to her home country.

There Was Not A Single Encourager or Spiritual Cheerleader In Her Life.

Have you ever experienced unbearable loneliness?

Ruth was "alone." She was the one with a desire to pursue a different Future.

▶ Her *Past* had no encouraging memories.

▶ Her *Present* had no encouraging motivation.

▶ Her *Future* was up to her alone.

The Uncommon Woman Motivates Herself When Others Are Uncaring.

RECOMMENDED INVESTMENTS:
The Uncommon Leader (Book/B-106/144 pg)
The Law of Recognition (Book/B-114/248 pg)
Seeds of Wisdom on Decision-Making (Book/B-125/32 pg)
Seeds of Wisdom on Motivating Yourself (Book/B-171/32 pg)
You Will Love Our Website..! WisdomOnline.com

⁓ 11 ⁓

THE UNCOMMON WOMAN IS WILLING TO INVEST EVERYTHING IN HER EXCELLENCE

A Tenacious Spirit Is Admirable.

Tenacious means *determined, persistent* and able to *commit* to a plan. What if there were no one in your life to speak a word of encouragement?

Would you persist?

Would you *stay* focused?

Will you *remain* bold and tenacious in pursuit of your *goals* and *dreams*...when *absolutely no one* really cares?

Ruth did.

Ruth had the *tenacity* that made her *unforgettable* and an *example* of The Uncommon Woman.

Tenacity will also make *You* The Uncommon Woman. Most of us appreciate expressions of encouragement...*daily*...*consistently*. It is wonderful when your mate is there to hold your hand through valleys of uncertainty. It is a precious thing when your little girl says, "Mommy, you can do anything!" But, what if you had no child to speak words of encouragement?

Every woman knows Seasons of Loneliness.

Moses must have known Seasons of Insignificance when he was in the desert.

David, the young shepherd boy, also felt disconnected from the great climate his brothers were enjoying. They experienced continual victories while serving in Saul's army.

It is wonderful to have encouragers around you. However if you are really going to produce significant fruit...you must learn the secret of motivating yourself.

Learn To Encourage Yourself By Accessing The Deepest Currents Flowing Within Your Own Heart.

If you keep waiting for everyone else—you will never move from where you are.

▶ Stay *enthusiastic.*
▶ Stay *energized.*
▶ Stay *motivated.*

Practice The Daily Habit of Self-Talk.

Your Words Are Powerful. You can motivate yourself and develop a consuming obsession for the specific Future you desire...by properly using your own words!

▶ Stop *complaining* that your mate is not interested in your personal dreams.
▶ Stop *whining* when your children show no interest in your personal goals.
▶ Stop holding *self-pity* parties. Nobody attends them anyway.

Embrace your Future. Do it with total *abandonment, joy* and *excitement.*

Make the determination that *Tomorrow will begin the best season of your life.*

The Uncommon Woman Is Willing To Invest Everything In Her Excellence.

⁓ 12 ⁓

THE UNCOMMON WOMAN IS RESPECTED FOR HER PERSONAL INTEGRITY

The Uncommon Woman Is Trustworthy.

The Biblical story of Ruth is fascinating.

Everyone knew about Ruth.

Boaz describes Ruth's reputation this way, "And Boaz answered and said unto her, It hath fully been shewed me, all that thou hast done unto thy mother in law since the death of thine husband: and how thou hast left thy father and thy mother, and the land of thy nativity, and art come unto a people which thou knewest not heretofore," (Ruth 2:11).

Later he said, "Blessed be thou of the Lord, my daughter: for thou hast shewed more kindness in the latter end than at the beginning, inasmuch as thou followedst not young men, whether poor or rich. And now, my daughter, fear not; I will do to thee all that thou requirest: for all the city of my people doth know that thou art a virtuous woman," (Ruth 3:10-11).

People talk...*good* and *bad...false* accusations and *true* assessments.

You Will Only Be Remembered In Life For Two Things: The Problems You Solve or The Ones You

Create.

People spoke well of Ruth. Her sacrificial attitude and dedication to preserve and maintain the life of her widowed mother-in-law was a known fact in the community. She had not even dated or bonded with any of the young men in the city—poor or rich.

Ruth's *total focus* was upon Naomi.

Character Is A Choice.

This truth had registered heavily upon the heart of Boaz who did not hesitate to respond to Ruth's pursuit of a relationship with him.

Ruth was commendable.

Are others able to commend you? "Let another man praise thee, and not thine own mouth; a stranger, and not thine own lips," (Proverbs 27:2).

The Uncommon Woman Is Respected For Her Personal Integrity.

RECOMMENDED INVESTMENTS:
Enjoying The Winning Life (Book/B-08/32 pg)
The Double Diamond Principle (Book/B-39/148 pg)
The Proverbs 31 Woman (Book/B-49/70 pg)
You Will Love Our Website..! WisdomOnline.com

～ 13 ～

THE UNCOMMON WOMAN IS AWARE HER REPUTATION IS MORE VALUABLE THAN MONEY

A Good Name Is Magnetic.

What do people think when they hear your name? "A good name is rather to be chosen than great riches, and loving favour rather than silver and gold," (Proverbs 22:1).

A good name is more magnetic than a strong fragrance. "A good name is better than precious ointment; and the day of death than the day of one's birth," (Ecclesiastes 7:1).

Several years ago, I arrived at the home of a young lady to take her to supper. As we were driving to the restaurant she remarked, "I had another date planned tonight, but I told him I had to visit a relative in the hospital."

She had *lied.* It *sickened* me. I had been excited about establishing a relationship with her only to find out within minutes that falsehood came naturally and *easily* to her. Obviously, if I continued in relationship with her, I would be the next victim on her list. It was the first and last date I had with her.

Develop integrity, whatever it takes. Carefully

examine each word that comes from your lips.

Refuse to brag on someone's singing if it is not praise worthy. Do not say things merely to encourage others. "Recompense to no man evil for evil. Provide things honest in the sight of all men," (Romans 12:17).

Never say anything insincere.

The compassion of Ruth was known. Before considering a relationship with a man, observe how he speaks to her mother. Note how well this *man* treats his *mother. Also consider* how he reacts to the struggle and heartaches of those less fortunate.

Ruth's purity and virtue were known even though many false accusations were hurled about during those days. *Reputations* of good people have been *stained* through the words of vindictive and spiritually violent people.

Remember Potiphar's wife? (See Genesis 39:7-20.) Joseph is not the only one who has walked upright before the Lord, only to have his reputation devastated after rejecting an immoral individual.

The entire town of Bethlehem knew of Ruth's obsession to serve, as well as her constant acts of kindness to her mother-in-law. It was said she treated her mother-in-law better than 7 sons would treat a mother. That kind of reputation is almost unheard of today.

Develop A Reputation of Kindness And Truth.

This does not mean you have to advertise your good deeds. Nor is it important to announce to the world all your acts of kindness and mercy.

God has a way of "letting your integrity be made known." What you are...will eventually be exposed.

Refuse To Be Discouraged When Others Misjudge Your Motives. Everyone has been misjudged at some time in their life. You will *always* have an adversary. "The words of the wicked are to lie in wait for blood: but the mouth of the upright shall deliver them," (Proverbs 12:6).

When a minister speaks on *prosperity*, he risks many accusations of *greed*. When he prays for the *sick*, he risks others calling him a *fraud*.

Your own family may misjudge your motives.

Any person who carries out your instructions may misinterpret your actions.

Your boss might misread you.

False Accusation Is The Last Stage Before Supernatural Promotion.

Take the time to discuss your position with those who are *genuinely* sincere. Do not waste your time and energy on those who are merely stirring up conflict.

The ministry of Jesus was constantly misjudged by others. "But when the Pharisees heard it, they said, This fellow doth not cast out devils, but by Beelzebub the prince of the devils," (Matthew 12:24).

Your *success* is on the other side of scorn and false accusations.

The Uncommon Woman Is Aware Her Reputation Is More Valuable Than Money.

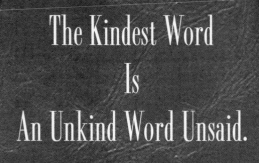

The Kindest Word
Is
An Unkind Word Unsaid.

-MIKE MURDOCK

Copyright © 2010 by Mike Murdock • Wisdom International
The Wisdom Center • 4051 Denton Hwy. • Ft. Worth, TX 76117

≈ 14 ≈

THE UNCOMMON WOMAN KNOWS THE IMPACT OF APPROPRIATE WORDS

Your Words Will Affect Your Success.

The Uncommon Woman places great importance upon speaking wise words. Your daily words and inner self-talk affect your success.

Dave Thomas, the beloved founder of the huge restaurant chain, Wendy's International, said, "Communication is the heart of success."

10 Incredible Ways Wise Words Can Affect Your Daily Success Rituals

1.   Wise Words Can Turn An Angry Person Into A Friend. "A soft answer turneth away wrath," (Proverbs 15:1).

2.   Wise Words Will Breathe Energy And Life Into Everything Around You. "A wholesome tongue is a tree of life," (Proverbs 15:4).

3.   Wise Words Can Energize And Motivate Your Own Life. "A man hath joy by the answer of his mouth: and a word spoken in due season, how good is it!" (Proverbs 15:23).

4.   Wise Words Decide Which Dreams Live And Which Dreams Die. "Death and life are in the power of the tongue: and they that love it shall eat the fruit thereof," (Proverbs 18:21).

5.   Wise Words Are As Important As Silver And Gold. "The tongue of the just is as choice silver," (Proverbs 10:20).

6.   Wise Words Can Get You Out of Trouble. "...but the mouth of the upright shall deliver them," (Proverbs 12:6).

7.   Wise Words Can Bring Health And Healing. "...the tongue of the wise is health," (Proverbs 12:18).

8.   Wise Words Can Open Doors To Powerful, Important And Influential Leaders. "Righteous lips are the delight of kings; and they love him that speaketh right," (Proverbs 16:13).

9.   Wise Words Can Cure Bitterness. "Pleasant words are as an honeycomb, sweet to the soul, and health to the bones," (Proverbs 16:24).

10. Wise Words Can Unlock A Financial Raise or Promotion. "A man's belly shall be satisfied with the fruit of his mouth; and with the increase of his lips shall he be filled," (Proverbs 18:20).

The Uncommon Woman Knows The Impact of Appropriate Words.

RECOMMENDED INVESTMENT:
The Hidden Power of Right Words (CD/WCPL-27)
You Will Love Our Website..! WisdomOnline.com

❧ 15 ❧

THE UNCOMMON WOMAN HAS THE SPIRIT OF A FINISHER

The Uncommon Woman Is A Finisher.

Completion creates pleasure. "The desire accomplished is sweet to the soul," (Proverbs 13:19).

Creativity is fun. It is always exciting to give *birth* to new ideas, think of new places to go or launch a new product. Real leaders though, *complete* things.

Real leaders are "Follow Through" people.

Jesus was 30 years old when He started His ministry and continued for three-and-one-half years. He touched many lives and performed many miracles. Jesus electrified the world through 12 men He trained. We know them as The Disciples.

Hidden in thousands of Scriptures is a Golden Principle that reveals His power.

On Crucifixion Day Jesus was taunted by thousands.

- ▶ A *Spear* pierced His side…
- ▶ *Spikes* were driven into His hands…
- ▶ *Thorns* 8 inches in length were crushed into His brow…

That moment was when He uttered perhaps the

greatest sentence ever spoken on earth: *"It is finished,"* (John 19:30). Jesus paid the price. He was the Lamb led to the slaughter. The sin of man could be forgiven.

The Plan Was Completed.

Jesus was the Chief Cornerstone. "And are built upon the foundation of the apostles and prophets, Jesus Christ Himself being the chief corner stone," (Ephesians 2:20).

The Prince of Peace had come. "For unto us a child is born, unto us a son is given: and the government shall be upon His shoulder: and His name shall be called Wonderful, Counsellor, The mighty God, The everlasting Father, The Prince of Peace," (Isaiah 9:6).

Our great High Priest, the Son of God, was our Golden Link to the God of Heaven. (See Hebrews 4:14.)

Uncommon Women Are Finishers.

Jesus Was A Finisher. He finished what He started. The bridge that linked man to God was complete. Man could now approach God without *fear* or *hesitation.*

The Apostle Paul Was A Finisher. "I have fought a good fight, I have finished my course, I have kept the faith," (2 Timothy 4:7).

Embrace The Spirit of A Finisher. "And ye shall be hated of all men for My name's sake: but he that endureth to the end shall be saved," (Matthew 10:22).

Start Completing Small Projects. Write that "thank you" note to your friend. Make those telephone calls. *Fight To Keep The Spirit of A Finisher.*

You are the *offspring* of a remarkable Creator.

Your *gifts* and *talents* have been placed within you by The Holy Spirit. You have been given the *Mind* of Christ.

Discover and celebrate the gifts that lie within you.

Find ways to use your gifts to *improve* others and help them to *achieve their* dreams and goals.

Go Where You Are Celebrated, Instead of Where You Are Tolerated.

Do not waste your energy trying to prove something to somebody else.

Your worth must be discerned.

Jesus knew this. Satan tempted Him. "If thou be the Son of God, command that these stones be made bread," (Matthew 4:3).

Jesus healed *deaf* ears...opened *blind* eyes...made the *lame* to walk...raised the *dead...sinners* were changed.

Yet, the jeers of the doubters continued to scream into His ears at His crucifixion, "And saying, Thou that destroyest the temple, and buildest it in three days, save Thyself. If Thou be the Son of God, come down from the cross," (Matthew 27:40).

What was the reaction of Jesus?

He was *confident* of His worth and *knew* His *purpose*. He refused to allow the taunts of ignorant men to change His plans.

The Price God Was Willing To Pay Reveals The Worth of The Product He Saw.

Your Assignment was decided before you were in your mother's womb. "Before I formed thee in the belly I knew thee; and before thou camest forth out of the womb I sanctified thee, and I ordained thee a prophet unto the nations," (Jeremiah 1:5).

God created you. He has always known the *invisible* purpose for which you were created.

Keep focused. You are not an accident waiting to

happen. "I will praise Thee; for I am fearfully and wonderfully made: marvellous are Thy works; and that my soul knoweth right well," (Psalm 139:14).

The Uncommon Woman Has The Spirit of A Finisher.

RECOMMENDED INVESTMENTS:
The Making of A Champion (Book/B-59/128 pg)
Born To Taste The Grapes (Book/B-65/32 pg)
Wisdom - God's Golden Key To Success (Book/B-71/78 pg)
You Will Love Our Website..! WisdomOnline.com

16

THE UNCOMMON WOMAN IS CONFIDENT IN HER DIFFERENCE

You Must Know Your Value.

You are not responsible for anything but an *honest effort* to please God. Something incredible resides inside you. Everything within you is *known, treasured* and *intended* to be fully *used* by your Creator. "My substance was not hid from Thee, when I was made in secret, and curiously wrought in the lowest parts of the earth," (Psalm 139:15).

Develop Confidence In Your Difference.

Your flaws do not necessarily prevent God from using you. Flaws exist to motivate your pursuit of Him. "Thine eyes did see my substance, yet being unperfect; and in Thy book all my members were written, which in continuance were fashioned, when as yet there was none of them," (Psalm 139:16).

Your Very Existence Excites God. "How precious also are Thy thoughts unto me, O God! how great is the sum of them! If I should count them, they are more in number than the sand: when I awake, I am still with Thee," (Psalm 139:17-18).

Picture an author ecstatic over his book. The book exists. The author created it. He is excited about it whether anyone else is or not.

Imagine a composer, exhilarated over a *completed* song. He knew its *beginning* and its *end*. Its very *sound* electrifies him.

Your Very Presence Energizes God. He saw your beginning and His desired conclusion. "For Thou hast created all things, and for Thy pleasure they are and were created," (Revelation 4:11).

God Is Looking At Something Within You That You Have Never Seen. "For man looketh on the outward appearance, but the Lord looketh on the heart," (1 Samuel 16:7).

God Is Looking At Something You Contain That You Have Not Yet Discovered. "For as the Heavens are higher than the earth, so are My ways higher than your ways, and My thoughts than your thoughts," (Isaiah 55:9).

God Will Tell You Secrets That Satan Will Never Hear. God is looking at something inside you that even satan *cannot* discern. (Read Job Chapters 1-3.)

The Uncommon Woman Is Confident In Her Difference.

≈ 17 ≈

THE UNCOMMON WOMAN IS A TROPHY OF THE GRACE OF GOD

―――――――▶●◀―――――――

You Are Moving Toward Excellence.

His mercies are not wasted on you. He has big plans. His forgiveness is not futile. "For we are His workmanship, created in Christ Jesus unto good works," (Ephesians 2:10).

▶ You May Be *Looking* At Your *Beginning.*
▶ God Is *Looking* At Your *End.*
▶ You May Be *Obsessed* With Your *Flaws.*
▶ God Is *Obsessed* With Your *Future.*
▶ You May Be *Focusing* On Your *Enemies.*
▶ God Is *Focusing* On Your *Eventuality.*

You Are A Trophy of His Grace.

God is not waiting for you to *Become* your Assignment. He awaits your *Discovery* of it. Do not bond with those who have not discovered the gift of God within you.

Their *focus* is *different.*

Their *conclusions* will be *inaccurate.*

Stay In The Presence of The One Who Created You.

You will always feel confident about yourself when you *stay* in His presence. He is looking at something in you that is remarkable. He planted something within you while you were yet in your mother's womb. (See Jeremiah 1:5.)

David understood this. King Saul and his brothers saw *brashness;* The Holy Spirit saw *boldness.* David's brothers saw *anger;* God saw a sense of *justice.* (See 1 Samuel 17:26-31.)

Joseph understood this.
His brothers saw *pride;*
God saw *thankfulness.*
The brothers saw *rivalry;*
God saw a *weapon.* (See Genesis 37:4-11.)

The opinions and observations of others are not your foundation for Greatness. God is looking at something inside you that they cannot see, refuse to see and may never be able to see.

➤ The brothers of *Jesus* did not grasp His Divinity. (See Matthew 12:47-50.)

➤ The brothers of *Joseph* misinterpreted him.

➤ The brothers of *David* saw a shepherd boy.

➤ The friends of *Job* could not discern the satanic scenario before his crisis. (See Job 1:8-12.)

➤ *Haman* could not even discern the nationality of Esther! (See Esther 7:3-6.) Only a fool ignores the desires of a king.

Few are ever accurate in their assessment of you. Your *flaws* are fewer than they imagine. Your Greatness is *greater* than they discern.

The Uncommon Woman Is A Trophy of The Grace of God.

RECOMMENDED INVESTMENT:
Seeds of Wisdom on Overcoming, Vol. 5 (Book/B-17/32 pg)
You Will Love Our Website..! WisdomOnline.com

~ 18 ~

THE UNCOMMON WOMAN TRUSTS THE HOLY SPIRIT TO BE HER SATISFIER

The Holy Spirit Satisfies.

The Holy Spirit is the only One Who has *accurately* assessed your Future. He sees the desires of your heart to become a Vessel of Honor. That is why He keeps *reaching, pursuing* and *developing* you in the midst of every attack and crisis.

▶ The *Seeker*...never gives up on you.

▶ The *Pursuer*...never stops looking for you.

▶ God never *changes* His plans toward you.

▶ God never quits *believing* in your Future.

He has decided the *conclusion* and is only awaiting your *discovery* of this truth.

God Sees Something In You That Others Do Not See. Stay continuously aware of this truth.

God sees something within you that keeps Him excited and involved. "Then Samuel took the horn of oil, and anointed him in the midst of his brethren: and the Spirit of the Lord came upon David from that day forward," (1 Samuel 16:13).

Those who know your value become qualified for access.

Those who do not ascribe proper value to your

Assignment are unqualified for admission into your world.

Do not open the door of your inner thought life to those who are unable to appreciate what God has chosen to do with your life and ministry.

Remember: *God Is Quite Aware of The Hidden Greatness Within You Others Do Not Yet Discern.*

The Uncommon Woman Trusts The Holy Spirit To Be Her Satisfier.

RECOMMENDED INVESTMENTS:
The Holy Spirit Handbook (Book/B-100/153 pg)
The 3 Most Important Things In Your Life (Book/B-101/240 pg)
You Will Love Our Website..! WisdomOnline.com

❧ 19 ❧

THE UNCOMMON WOMAN IS A PROBLEM-SOLVER

The Uncommon Woman Solves Problems.

Someone needs you. "Greater love hath no man than this, that a man lay down his life for his friends," (John 15:13).

Successful People Are Simply Problem-Solvers.

Your success and happiness in life depends on your *willingness* to help others solve their problems.

▶ Attorneys solve *legal* problems.

▶ Doctors solve *medical* problems.

▶ Mechanics solve *vehicle* problems.

The Uncommon Woman Identifies What She Possesses That Others Need.

Jesus is our perfect example.

Jesus was a Problem-Solver.

Thousands were burdened with guilt because of their sins. Jesus offered forgiveness.

Thousands were spiritually starved. He said, "I am the Bread of Life."

Hundreds had bodies riddled with sickness and disease. Jesus "went about doing good, and healing all that were oppressed of the devil; for God was with Him," (Acts 10:38). Many were possessed with evil spirits.

Jesus had something others needed.

He *solved* their problems.

Jesus set them free. That is why thousands sat for days as He taught them from the Laws of God and how to have extraordinary relationships.

Consider The Products Jesus Has To Offer:

▶ Eternal Life

▶ Everlasting Joy

▶ Inner Peace

▶ Forgiveness

▶ Healing

▶ Health

▶ Financial Freedom

Take an inventory of yourself.

What do you have to offer someone else?

What do you enjoy doing?

What would you attempt to do if you knew it was impossible to fail?

Always Identify What You Possess That...Others Need.

The Uncommon Woman Is A Problem-Solver.

RECOMMENDED INVESTMENTS:
7 Rewards of Problem Solving (Book/B-118/32 pg)
7 Signposts To Your Assignment (Book/B-122/32 pg)
You Will Love Our Website..! WisdomOnline.com

≈ 20 ≈

THE UNCOMMON WOMAN IS IRREPLACEABLE

You Are Irreplaceable In Your Assignment.

Jonah revealed this when God used the wind and a huge fish to motivate him. Nobody was chosen to "replace" him.

Everything God Makes Is A Solution To A Problem.

God wanted a love relationship...He created Adam.

Adam was lonely...God created Eve.

This is the Golden Thread that links creation.

Think of your contribution to another as an Assignment from God.

▶ A Lawyer is assigned to his *client.*

▶ A Wife is assigned to her *husband.*

▶ Parents are assigned to their *children.*

▶ A Secretary is assigned to her *boss.*

Your Assignment Is Always To A Person or A People. For example, Moses was assigned to the Israelites. Aaron was assigned to Moses.

Your Assignment Will Always Solve A Problem. Your life is a solution to someone in trouble. Find those who need you. Discover what you have to offer and build your life around that contribution.

7 *Qualities of The Uncommon Woman*

1.   The Uncommon Woman Sees What Others Do Not See.
2.   The Uncommon Woman Is Not Afraid To Speak Truth.
3.   The Uncommon Woman Thinks What Others Do Not Take The Time To Think.
4.   The Uncommon Woman Gives People What They Need Instead of What They Want.
5.   The Uncommon Woman Allows Time For Changes.
6.   The Uncommon Woman Believes In People And Their Uniqueness.
7.   The Uncommon Woman Is Able To Focus On Real Life Issues.

The Uncommon Woman Is Irreplaceable.

RECOMMENDED INVESTMENTS:
The Law of Recognition (Book/B-114/247 pg)
The Wisdom Commentary, Vol. 1 (Book/B-136/256 pg)
You Will Love Our Website..! WisdomOnline.com

≈ 21 ≈

THE UNCOMMON WOMAN PROTECTS AND NURTURES WORTHY RELATIONSHIPS

━━━━▶➤◦◀━━━━

Relationships Grow Weeds or Flowers.
Every friendship has an *impact* in your life.
Every relationship must be clearly *defined* and *understood* by both parties.

25 Facts About Relationships

1. Your Choice of Friends Affects Your Future.

2. Every Relationship Feeds Your Weakness or Nurtures Your Strength.

3. Every Friendship Is Comfortable With Your Present or Compatible With Your Future.

4. Every Relationship Is A Current That Sweeps You Toward Your Assignment or Moves You Away From It.

5. Some Relationships Can Cause You Irreparable Damage.

6. Some Relationships Multiply Your Wisdom.

7. The Purpose of Wisdom Is To Disconnect You From Wrong People.

8. Your Future Is Determined By The People You Permit Near You.

9. When Satan Wants To *Destroy* You, He Puts A Person In Your Life.

10. When God Wants To *Promote* You, He Puts A Person In Your Life.

11. Those Who Are Fighting Against God Will Fight Against The God *In You.*

12. Those Who Despise Obedience To God Will Despise *Your* Obedience To God.

13. Those Who Desire God Will Recognize The God In You.

14. Those Who Do Not Increase You Will Inevitably Decrease You.

15. Those Who Do Not Make Deposits Into You Will Eventually Make Withdrawals From You.

16. Each Relationship Will Abort or Advance Your Assignment.

17. The Holy Spirit Alone Can Direct You To The Right People Who Will Assist You In Completing Your Assignment.

18. No Relationship Is Insignificant.

19. Intimacy Should Be *Earned,* Not Freely Given.

20. Intimacy Should Be The Reward For *Proven* Loyalty.

21. True Friendship Is A *Gift,* Never A Demanded Requirement.

22. When *Wrong* People Leave Your Life, Wrong Things *Stop* Happening.

23. When *Right* People Enter Your Life, *Right Things* Begin To Happen.

24. If You Fail To Guard Your Own Life, You Are Like A City Without Walls.

25. Failure Occurs When The Wrong Person Gets Too Close.
One of The Greatest Gifts God Can Give You Other Than Himself Is A Friend.

Desire for Relationship is present from birth.

However, relationships bring challenges with them.

The Uncommon Woman is aware of the importance of *protecting* her relationships.

A True Friend

▶ A True Friend will remain consistent during times of upheavals.
▶ A True Friend is truthful...even when the truth hurts.
▶ A True Friend is accessible during times of loneliness and heartache.
▶ A True Friend will increase your strength during adversity.
▶ A True Friend will stay loyal during crisis.

A True Friendship begins as a Seed requiring constant watering, nurturing and protection.

Much of modern communication is through e-mail. Twitter is a fun entry into the social networking environment.

Meaningful Conversation...births every significant change in your life.

3 Insights To Quality Conversation

1. Be Concise When You Speak To Others.
Your best qualities will surface in the presence of quality people. Do not ramble. Do not use 10 words when 5 will suffice.

2. Always Be Where You Are. When you are engaged in conversation with someone, totally focus on that conversation. Later you will not have to reflect back with regret about that conversation. This type of sharpened focus during conversation can prevent unnecessary cases of misjudgment created by miscommunication.

3. Concentrate Upon Engaging In More Creative Conversation. I was watching television news concerning the awful oil spill in the Gulf of Mexico. Members of each political party were putting forth their "talking points." I was pleased by the direct assessment offered by a fisherman affected by the tragedy. He spoke with both eloquence and passion. These factors made his speech memorable. Simply put, people are much more likely to remember a well-spoken phrase.

Quality Relationships Must Be Treasured.

Success in life never arrives at the address of those who have no dreams or goals. The attention of The Uncommon Woman remains passionately focused upon her goals. Those who stir her passion toward the desires of her heart are always welcome in her life.

Treasure any relationship that generates energy and enthusiasm toward achieving your dreams and goals.

The Uncommon Woman Protects And Nurtures Worthy Relationships.

22

THE UNCOMMON WOMAN EXUDES GRATITUDE

Appreciative Women Are Magnetic.

It is interesting to note the reaction of Ruth when Boaz gave her permission to stay and glean barley from his fields.

She thanked him warmly. "Then she fell on her face, and bowed herself to the ground, and said unto him, Why have I found grace in thine eyes, that thou shouldest take knowledge of me, seeing I am a stranger? And Boaz answered and said unto her, It hath fully been shewed me, all that thou hast done unto thy mother in law since the death of thine husband: and how thou hast left thy father and thy mother, and the land of thy nativity, and art come unto a people which thou knewest not heretofore," (Ruth 2:10-11).

Verse 13 reveals that Ruth spoke detailed words of appreciation for the favor Boaz directed her way. "Then she said, Let me find favour in thy sight, my lord; for that thou hast comforted me, and for that thou hast spoken friendly unto thine handmaid, though I be not like unto one of thine handmaidens," (Ruth 2:13).

Ruth did not assume this unusual display of kindness was owed to her. She did not ask for *extra* favor. She *valued* the smallest crumb of barley left in her behalf.

Ruth was *appreciative* and *attentive.* Many relationships are lost due to inattention and insensitivity.

The Uncommon Woman is attentive to and focused upon the needs of friends. She is appreciative of the blessings others release into her life.

One of the best character traits of the uncommon woman is a thankful heart. She exudes gratitude continuously. The word 'appreciative' means, "Showing appreciation of someone or for something; to be grateful."

Appreciative Women Have 'Magnetism'.

Their amazing ability to value acts of kindness inspires others and makes them want to perform accordingly.

Years ago, Jessica was a beautiful little 9 year-old girl in Minneapolis, Minnesota. She was so articulate, expressive and appreciative.

Every time I did something special for her, she looked up with her big beautiful eyes and the biggest smile you could imagine, and said, "Oh, thank you so very much!"

The beautiful expressions of appreciation that flowed through Jessica made her magnetic!

It is this *attitude* of *appreciation* that makes children so delightful and makes us want to produce for them.

Often it is said, that Christmas is for children. They appreciate Christmas in a way that adults cannot seem to do. Each year I find myself wondering, "Why do we not enjoy Christmas as they do?"

Children *appreciate.*

They *celebrate the great event* of gift giving.

For many of us Christmas is almost just another day. After receiving so many gifts and blessings over a long period of time, our ability to appreciate seems to have deteriorated and diminished.

Place value on what you have in your personal life...especially in your home. Do not take for granted that your husband is "supposed to bring home the paycheck." Do not assume that it is "a woman's place" to clean up the house and prepare the meals.

Appreciation of those around you...will make you unforgettable. Ask The Holy Spirit to help you find ways to express your appreciation to others.

No Relationship Is Insignificant In Your Life.

Friendship with one *wrong* person can destroy you forever. *Worthy* relationships will release intimacy and *favor* into your life.

8 Ways To Express Appreciation

1. Do It Verbally. Speak kind words of appreciation.

2. Do It Privately. When no one else is around, be gentle in expressing your true appreciation and gratefulness.

3. Do It Publicly. Others need to hear that you appreciate how God has blessed you.

4. Do It Often. Not just once a year at a birthday or an anniversary.

5. Do It Generously. Go the extra mile when buying a gift for someone you love and appreciate.

6. Do It Thoughtfully. One of my closest friends in Sarasota, Florida, sent me two books recently.

What types of books? The author that he knows I love to read. He placed careful thought into the purchase of my gift.

7.   Do It Quickly. If someone has blessed your life significantly, do not wait several months or years to express it. Develop the *habit* of responding to an act of kindness within 72 hours.

8.   Do It Cheerfully.   When you express appreciation, do not do it grudgingly as if it is a painful effort.

Exude Gratitude *Continuously.*

The Uncommon Woman Exudes Gratitude.

RECOMMENDED INVESTMENTS:
Thirty-One Secrets of An Unforgettable Woman (Book/B-57/140 pg)
The Wisdom Commentary, Vol. 3 (Book/B-228/222 pg)
You Will Love Our Website..! WisdomOnline.com

❧ 23 ❧

THE UNCOMMON WOMAN IS SPONTANEOUS AND WILLING TO CHANGE

Spontaneity Is A Valuable Character Trait.

Ruth willingly left her heathen family in Moab and went to Bethlehem with Naomi, where she met and married Boaz, a *financial* giant of the community. (See Ruth 1:16-19, 4:13.)

It is normal to move toward those who are easily accessible. Sometimes, you have to go somewhere you have never been before you taste the *extraordinary* success you want to experience.

Yes, it is acceptable to ask The Holy Spirit to grant you access to rare achievers. However, it is important to be willing to start small.

Little Things Matter

Small hinges swing huge doors.

Small keys *unlock* vaults with millions of dollars.

A little steering determines the direction of a huge semi-truck.

One small finger dialing the telephone can begin a business transaction of one billion dollars.

Many will not become The Uncommon Woman because they want their *beginning* to be spectacular.

Never despise small beginnings. "For who hath despised the day of small things?" (Zechariah 4:10).

There is a fascinating story in the Bible of a man who was a leper. His name was Naaman. He was the commanding General of Syria. He went to the house of Elisha, the prophet to ask for healing. Elisha sent him a simple instruction to go wash in the Jordan River 7 times.

Naaman was infuriated. He had a different mental picture of how his healing would occur. One of his servants made an interesting statement, "My father, if the prophet had bid thee do some great thing, wouldest thou not have done it? how much rather then, when he saith to thee, Wash, and be clean?" (2 Kings 5:13).

The Assignment from Elisha was simple, clear and direct. "Naaman, Go! Wash in the Jordan River 7 times!"

When you are willing to do the simple, the Supernatural occurs.

Small Beginnings Often Have Great Endings

Jesus understood this principle.

He was born in a stable, in a small town of Bethlehem.

His beginning did not matter to Him.

He *knew* His *Destiny*.

He was aware of the greatness of His *destination*.

One of His greatest statements ever was, "He that

is faithful in that which is least is faithful also in much: and he that is unjust in the least is unjust also in much," (Luke 16:10).

Attention To Details Produces Excellence

The difference between *Extraordinary* Champions and Losers is the attention to detail.

Do not allow yourself to feel insignificant in what appears to be small acts of obedience while giving birth to your Assignment.

One of the great evangelists of our day began his ministry duplicating tapes for his mentor. Hour after hour, day after day, he sat and duplicated tapes. As he worked, he listened intently to each tape as it recorded.

He *assisted.*

He *listened.*

He *learned.*

He *ministered.*

He *served.*

It was the *beginning* of a significant ministry.

Ruth began life as a Moabite heathen girl. Her attention to the small details of her Assignment, (Naomi), positioned her as the great-grandmother of David and ushered in the lineage of Jesus. (See Ruth 4:13, 21-22.)

Abigail brought lunch to the starving man, David, and later became his wife. (See 1 Samuel 25:10-42.)

When Jesus wanted to produce a great miracle, He always gave a *small* instruction.

Little things mattered to Him.

Little things *still* matter to Him.

Notice the small, *seemingly* insignificant

instructions that Jesus gave. Looking back they almost seemed ridiculous. Some might think these were instructions given to children, but they were given to grown, *mature* adults.

Jesus spoke to the blind man, "And said unto him, Go, wash in the pool of Siloam, (which is by interpretation, Sent.) He went his way therefore, and washed, and came seeing," (John 9:7).

This *small* instruction produced a *big* miracle. Yes, a man was healed from a lifetime of blindness.

Another example is when Jesus gave an instruction to a group of weary fishermen, "Now when He had left speaking, He said unto Simon, Launch out into the deep, and let down your nets for a draught," (Luke 5:4).

Obedience to this simple command produced the greatest catch of fish the disciples had ever gathered.

The first miracle Jesus performed was at a wedding in Cana, "Jesus saith unto them, Fill the waterpots with water. And they filled them up to the brim," (John 2:7). It produced the greatest wine anyone had ever tasted.

The Apostle Mark recorded the powerful story of a healing that came about because of an obeyed instruction. "I say unto thee, Arise, and take up thy bed, and go thy way into thine house," (Mark 2:11).

What was the result? A paralyzed man immediately arose, took up his bed and started walking. The result was that "many glorified God." This miracle was produced by obedience to a simple instruction.

Remember the story of the lad and his lunch?

These words were spoken regarding the 5 loaves and 2 fishes, the lunch of a lad. "He said, Bring them hither to Me," (Matthew 14:18). What happened afterwards has been preached around the world... *thousands* were fed.

Miraculously, each of the 12 disciples had a basketful of leftovers to take home!

Great Miracles Do Not Require Great Instructions.
Great Miracles Require Obeyed Instructions.

A student in Bible college sits in chapel daily awaiting a neon sign in the Heavens declaring, "Bob, go to Calcutta, India."

It never happens.

Why? Bob has not obeyed the *first* instruction. "Bob, go to the prayer room at 7:00 a.m."

Obedience Turns A Common Instruction Into An Uncommon Miracle.

God does not give great instructions to great women. God gives *Uncommon* Instructions to *common* women.

Greatness Is Birthed When A Spirit-Given Instruction Is Obeyed. "If ye be willing and obedient, ye shall eat the good of the land," (Isaiah 1:19).

Nothing you do today will be small in the eyes of God. Be willing to go where you have never been before, and be willing to start small.

The Uncommon Woman Is Spontaneous And Willing To Change.

When You Replay
The Past,
You Poison
The Present.

-MIKE MURDOCK

Copyright © 2010 by Mike Murdock • Wisdom International
The Wisdom Center • 4051 Denton Hwy. • Ft. Worth, TX 76117

~ 24 ~

THE UNCOMMON WOMAN GRACIOUSLY EXITS RELATIONSHIPS

Relationships Do Not Last Forever.

Some relationships are seasonal. This is the reason it is important to properly *exit* every door of friendship.

It is important you exit your *present* season *correctly* so you can enter the next season of your life with joy.

Jesus finished His work on earth. He cried out from the cross, "It is finished!" (See John 19:30.) Salvation was complete. Redemption took place when Jesus paid the price for the sins of man.

Three days later, the resurrection would take place. Jesus returned to the Father where He is still making intercession for you and me.

Jesus, The Example of All Examples, finished properly...with the *approval* of the Father.

When Solomon finished the temple...it was an incredible feat. The value of his temple today is over $500 billion. Because he completed what he started, King Solomon was respected, pursued and celebrated. (See 2 Chronicles 7:11.)

Greatness Is Simply Fulfilling God's Expectations of You.

Paul fought a good fight, stayed on course and most importantly...*finished* the race. Because of this Paul was a success in the eyes of God. He made his exit from his earthly ministry with *dignity, grace* and *passion.* (See 2 Timothy 4:7.)

Your Life is a collection of *Beginnings.*

Your Life is also a collection of *Exits.*

It is unlikely you will *stay* in your present job. Someday you will leave your present position. Your supervisor *today* could be another acquaintance in your life, next year. *Close Every Relationship With Dignity.*

8 Keys To Remember When A Relationship Is Ending

1. Close Every Door Gently. Do not slam doors. Do not kick doors. They are doors through which you may need to return in the Future. The *attitude* of your exit determines if you can ever walk through that door again. "A soft answer turneth away wrath: but grievous words stir up anger," (Proverbs 15:1).

2. Close Doors With Forgiveness. Unforgiveness is like a poisonous cancer that will destroy you from within. Permit God to do the penalizing or correcting of others. Like Joseph, recognize that the ultimate plan of God will bring promotion. (See Romans 8:28.)

3. Close Doors With Kindness. If your fiancée leaves you with cutting and bitter words, thank The Holy Spirit for *salvaging* you. Perhaps he was not your Uncommon Man after all.

4. Close Every Door With Promises Fulfilled. Do not leave your job until you have finished what you promised. Complete every vow...whatever the cost. Integrity is easy to test. Simply ask yourself, "Did I fulfill my promise?" (Read Ecclesiastes 5:4-5.)

When people lose you in the forest of words, apply this principle of vow fulfillment. *Refuse to accuse, blame or complain.* This principle reveals everything you need to know about a person's integrity.

5. Close Every Door With Integrity. Few will do it. People are rarely angry for the reason they tell you. The trap of deception is deadly. It begins when you deceive yourself. Too often those around you will walk through this same door of deception. Always be honest to others about the reason for the doors closing.

It is not necessary to give *every* detail.

It is important the details you give are *accurate.*

6. Close Every Door With Courage. It is not always easy to close a door required by The Holy Spirit. Closing that door may take uncommon courage in facing the Future without that person. Remember The Precious Holy Spirit will never leave you nor forsake you. (See John 14:16.) He both *opens* and *closes* doors. *The Holy Spirit is The Bridge to every person in your Future.*

7. Close Every Door With Expectation of Promotion. "For promotion cometh neither from the east, nor from the west, nor from the south. But God is the judge: He putteth down one, and setteth up another," (Psalm 75:6-7).

8. Close Every Door By The Timing of The Holy Spirit. Do not close it in a fit of anger or because of a misunderstanding. Do not close it because someone *recommends* that you exit. *Know the timing of God.*

A young man sat in my kitchen a few weeks ago who wanted a position in my ministry. I was quite concerned. I asked him about his relationship with his previous boss, who was a preacher friend of mine. He kept avoiding the issue. In fact, I had to ask him the question several times before, I got a *partial* answer.

At the end of the conversation, he explained he was in a financial dilemma because he had left his last job before securing another.

Patiently, I explained to him how foolish such an action was. *If God were moving the young man, He would also tell him the place he was to go.*

God always brings you out of a place to take you into another place. Close every door with God's timing.

Remember to close doors *gently,* news will travel... *good news.*

The Uncommon Woman Graciously Exits Relationships.

RECOMMENDED INVESTMENTS:
Seeds of Wisdom on Relationships (Book/B-14/32 pg)
Thirty-One Secrets of An Unforgettable Woman (Book/B-57/140 pg)
You Will Love Our Website..! WisdomOnline.com

❧ 25 ❧

THE UNCOMMON WOMAN PERMITS YESTERDAY TO DIE

Move Beyond The Scars of Yesterday.

We have all experienced pain and have yesterdays we want to forget. Misfortune is a part of life. This may not sound too spiritual but, "Over is over." Part of choosing to move forward with your life involves the decision to allow Yesterday to die.

Stop Signs On Your Pathway To Victory

- ▶ *Stop* talking about your limited education.
- ▶ *Stop* complaining that your family is poor.
- ▶ *Stop* repeating stories of your failures.
- ▶ *Stop* pointing your finger at your boss.
- ▶ *Stop* advertising your pain.
- ▶ *Stop* meditating on your flaws.

Everyone has limitations.

Each of us is handicapped in some way... *physically, emotionally, mentally* or *spiritually.*

Your Work Should Produce Your Joy. "And also that every man should eat and drink, and enjoy the good of all his labour, it is the gift of God," (Ecclesiastes 3:13).

Your Joy Is Determined By Doing What You Love. Jesus associated with fishermen and talked to tax collectors. Doctors, lawyers and religious leaders were in His life daily, but He never wavered from His focus. The Bible says that "God anointed Jesus of Nazareth with the Holy Ghost and with power: Who went about doing good, and healing all that were oppressed of the devil; for God was with Him," (Acts 10:38).

Jesus knew His mission.

Some people accept jobs because they are convenient or close to their home. One man told me he had spent his entire life working on a job that made him miserable.

I asked. "Why then have you worked there for 27 years?" He replied. "It is only 10 minutes from my house, and in 3 years, I will receive a gold watch. I do not want to leave too early and miss my gold watch." What a high price to pay. Ask yourself the following questions:

▶ What do you love to do?
▶ What do you love to talk about?
▶ What would you rather hear about more than anything else on earth?
▶ What would you do with your life if money were not a factor?
▶ What do you do best of all?

Empty your Future of bad memories and concentrate on recreating your Future.

Make the decision to rise above the stigma attached to any questionable events in your Past.

Ruth did...she refused to become the living link between the *Past* and her *Future*. She abandoned *empty* relationships of her Past.

Ruth was a rare person who knew when she had exhausted the benefits of her *present* season.

The Bible contains an illustration of the damage that can be produced from unproductive relationships. This example is drawn from the life of the great patriarch, Abraham, who insisted on bringing Lot, his nephew, with him into the Future God had prepared.

Some People Are Distractions.

Lot was a distraction. Most of Abraham's continual problems can be traced to the ongoing *presence* of Lot.

God told Abraham to leave his kinfolk and move to a different territory.

However, Abraham insisted on bringing someone with whom he was comfortable. He did so to the *detriment* of his Future.

Yesterday People Will Rarely Enjoy Your God-Ordained Future.

It is natural to want to bring those close to you into the chapters of your Future success.

Hear this unpleasant truth…*few will qualify.*

Your Future must be earned…it is *not* guaranteed.

Bringing *Yesterday* people into the Future is like expecting old wineskins to hold the new wine that is coming *Tomorrow.*

This simply will not work.

You have exhausted the *benefits* of Yesterday so *prepare to enter your Future without attempting to bring Yesterday people along.*

God will send the right associations to you.

You are not *forfeiting* loyalty.

He has scheduled outstanding *Divine Connections* beyond your wildest dreams. Yesterday can be a *reservoir* of Wisdom and information for you to draw upon.

You are not forgetting the precious lives God used mightily for your *continued* survival and success.

You must disconnect from your pain-filled past. Refuse to abort your Future joys and victories by *replaying* the memories of Yesterday's painful experiences.

▶ Move Away From Yesterday.
▶ Refuse To Waste Energy On The Restoration of Your Past.
▶ Rebuild By Focusing On Your Future.

Few made greater mistakes than Paul, yet he refused to forfeit his Future by wallowing in the tears of his Past.

Many were cast into *prison*...Christians were *murdered*...because of Paul.

The young lawyer held the coats of those who stoned the great deacon, Stephen.

His *mistakes* were over.

His *sins* were behind him.

His *name* had been changed.

Eventually, you will need to make a major decision in your life to *totally abandon* your memories, and pour your energy into the *palace* of your Future.

Look For Divinely Created Advantage.

Every season in your life will contain advantages. Seek The Holy Spirit's direction concerning the *Divine* purposes of God in every situation in your life.

Allow Him to reveal the blessing involved in each relationship regardless of the length of time involved.

Discern the *Divine* purpose of God in every relationship. Refuse to waste time on extended conversations with those to whom you are not spiritually connected.

Think about it. Would you keep chewing the same mouthful of food for 3 hours? *No.*

Would you keep reading the same page of a book for 3 days? *No.*

Would you leave a broken record on in the same groove replaying the same note repeatedly for several hours? *Of course not!*

When something is finished...*it is finished.*

▶ *Discern* it.

▶ *Look* for it.

▶ *Recognize* it.

Consistently be intuitive and discerning when a specific season in your life has concluded. Then, move *quickly* and *expectantly* to the next season God has arranged for you.

The Uncommon Woman Permits Yesterday To Die.

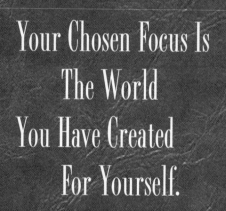

Your Chosen Focus Is
The World
You Have Created
For Yourself.

-MIKE MURDOCK

Copyright © 2010 by Mike Murdock • Wisdom International
The Wisdom Center • 4051 Denton Hwy. • Ft. Worth, TX 76117

≈ 26 ≈

THE UNCOMMON WOMAN STAYS IN THE CENTER OF HER EXPERTISE

Protect Your Passion At All Costs.

What you love is a clue to your calling and talent. Pour all of yourself into your leadership role. "And whatsoever ye do, do it heartily, as to the Lord, and not unto men," (Colossians 3:23).

The Uncommon Woman Fights For One Focus.

Jesus focused on following the instructions of His Father. He healed the sick. He came to make people successful, to restore their lives to full fellowship with His Heavenly Father. Jesus did all these things because He obeyed a single word from His Father. "Go!"

Your Obsession Toward Becoming The Uncommon Woman Will Cost You...Everything.

That Obsession took Jesus to the cross. It carried Him to the crucifixion.

Jesus was obsessed with the salvation of humanity...and He succeeded.

Do you dread going to work every morning?

Do you anxiously look at the clock toward closing time each afternoon?

Do you find your mind wandering throughout the

day?

Do your thoughts drift towards other places or things you would rather be doing?

If so, you will probably not have success at what you are presently doing.

Find something that consumes you, something that is worthy of building your entire life around.

Empty yourself into something you love.

Focusing On Your Future Masters Your Past.

Do What You Do Best

Stay in the center of what you love most. "Brethren, I count not myself to have apprehended: but this one thing I do, forgetting those things which are behind, and reaching forth unto those things which are before, I press toward the mark for the prize of the high calling of God in Christ Jesus," (Philippians 3:13-14).

Are you having self-doubts today?

Are your thoughts plagued by the seemingly restrictions of *limited* education...your father dying when you were young...an *alcoholic* parent...*guilt* over a serious mistake you made in your teenage years?

Such thoughts are common to all believers. *You must remember that your Past is over.*

Protect Your Passion At All Costs.

One of the best ways of doing this is doing what God has called you to do. It is only by focusing on your Assignment that you can maintain the focus that is needed for the work at hand.

The Uncommon Woman Stays In The Center of Her Expertise.

❧ 27 ❧

THE UNCOMMON WOMAN DEVELOPS SUCCESS HABITS

Habit Is A Misunderstood Word.

For many, the word "habit" carries with it a negative connotation.

But, habit can be a good thing.

Basketball Superstar Larry Bird shot 100 free throws at the conclusion of practice each day.

It was a *Success Habit.*

Cosmetics giant Mary Kay Ash habitually spent time organizing her day.

Daily prayer is a habit that still sustains my 93 year old father, the Rev. J. E. Murdock.

Developing New Habits Is A Challenge.

In order to develop a new series of success habits, you simply must have an *awakening* within you of how great your life can truly become.

However, getting to this zone of uncommon success will require changes…new habits to develop and adapt. With determination and tenacity, you can become The Uncommon Woman.

3 Truths About Habits

▶ You cannot change your life until you change

your *Habits*.
- ▶ You cannot change your Habits until you change your *Dream*.
- ▶ You will not change your Dream until you become dissatisfied with your *Present*.

In California, a powerful spiritual leader awakens at 5:30 a.m. each day. He has followed this routine for years. He prays from 5:30 a.m. to 6:30 a.m. This is his daily habit—*The Success Habit* that has unlocked an unforgettable anointing for teaching. He *lives* and *breathes* the atmosphere of *success*. Is it a mystery? Not really.

Habit is the most misunderstood word in the English language. When someone talks about habits, everyone thinks about drugs, alcohol or smoking. They think habit is a word connected to something evil, deteriorating or deadly.

Habit is a gift from God enabling us to succeed. Habit is a good word, a God word.

Habit simply means that when you do something twice, it becomes easier.

Personal Hygiene Habits increase your *health, self-confidence* and *social influence*.

Conversation Habits strengthen *integrity, relationships* and build *self-confidence*.

Financial Habits can create uncommon *increase*. Your spending habits are creating a *secure* financial Future or *destroying* it completely. A friend of mine told me that a simple saving of $100 invested in mutual funds, every month...would result in a baby becoming a millionaire at 20 years old. *Habits Create Paupers or Millionaires*.

Health Habits define who you are today. Your habits have created your present physical condition.

Whether you are overweight, unhealthy or uncommonly strong, what you keep eating daily is creating the You-In-The-Future. What you eat is *increasing* or *decreasing* your health.

Desires Birth Habits. Some who have smoked for 40 years quit in a week when the doctor revealed that they were standing at the door of death.

Discipline is different than habit. God did not create us to be creatures of discipline but creatures of habit.

The Purpose of Discipline Is To Birth A Habit. Psychologists say that when you perform an act for 21 consecutive days without fail, it will become a habit. Habits create a Future you will love or hate.

Habit Is The Child of Purpose, Destiny And Desire. Let me give you an example.

When Mohammed Ali, the great boxer, believed that destiny and God had determined his Future, that he would be the greatest boxer on earth, his habits *changed.* He arose earlier and his *workouts* became more intense. His *conversation* style changed, and yes, he even changed his name!

The Uncommon Woman Develops Success Habits.

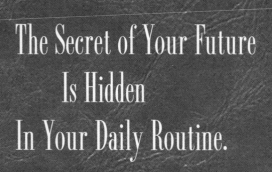

The Secret of Your Future
Is Hidden
In Your Daily Routine.

-MIKE MURDOCK

Copyright © 2010 by Mike Murdock • Wisdom International
The Wisdom Center • 4051 Denton Hwy. • Ft. Worth, TX 76117

❧ 28 ❧

THE UNCOMMON WOMAN DEVELOPS HER DAILY SUCCESS ROUTINE

Your Habits Decide Your Future.
Your habits are the result of what you believe you deserve to have and possess.

Wisdom Keys For The Uncommon Woman To Use In Her Daily Success Routine

▶ *You Do Not Decide Your Future, You Decide The Habits That Determine Your Future.*
▶ *What You Do Daily Is Deciding What You Are Becoming Permanently.*
▶ *Nothing Will Ever Dominate Your Life Unless It Happens Daily.*
▶ *You Cannot Change Your Life Until You Change Something You Keep Doing...Daily.*
▶ *You Can Trace The Failure of Every Woman To Something She Permitted To Occur Daily In Her Life, Body or Her Mind.*
▶ *You Can Trace Uncommon Success To Habits That Were Created...A Daily Success Routine.*
▶ *Your Habits Are Creating Increase or Decrease.*

▶ *Your Habits Are Being Strengthened or Changed By The Friends You Permit Daily Close To You.*

▶ *What You Keep Looking At Is Deciding Where You Will Go.*

▶ *Gaze Only Upon That Which You Desire In Your Future.*

▶ *You Will Always Move Toward The Dominant Picture In Your Mind.* That is why it is important that you place pictures around you of the things you desire to move toward.

▶ *A Failure Routine Can Be Changed Into A Success Routine Within 21 Days.*

▶ *What You Keep Doing Daily Is Creating The Future You Have Always Wanted or The Future You Dread.*

▶ *Your Money Habits Are Making You A Pauper or A Millionaire.*

The Ancient Writings depict several photographs of people who developed success habits and routines.

1) *Jesus* went regularly to the synagogue.
2) *David* prayed 7 times each day.
3) *Daniel* prayed 3 times each day.
4) *Zacharias* offered up sacrifices "...as was his custom."

It Is Almost Impossible To Fail When Your Daily Success Routine Begins With The First Hour of Every Day In The Presence of God.

One of the most famous businesswomen on earth lived here in Dallas, Texas. She was worth over 300 million dollars personally at the time of her death. The business she founded is worth over two billion today.

The Great Lady Had A Daily Success Routine.

Since 1962, she would write her daily plan on a sheet of paper. She listed 6 tasks for the day.

She worked on her list starting with the *first* and continued until all 6 goals were *completed.*

She believed that one of The Master Keys to her *Uncommon Success* was this constant and consistent daily habit.

Planning was a big part of her daily routine.

A former Presidential Chief-of-Staff revealed part of his Daily Success Routine. The first thing he did every morning and the last thing he did every night was to plan the day of the President.

It was his habit.

One of the wealthiest athletes in history revealed a few weeks ago that the morning after he won the heavyweight championship of the world, he was back in his gym! He was faithful to his *Daily Success Routine*…the morning after he had earned millions of dollars within minutes.

He knew and had decided for his life, the daily habits *necessary* to create the Future he loved.

One famous Hall of Fame baseball pitcher pitched his seventh no-hitter. Afterwards, reporters found him in the locker room doing what he always did—riding a stationary bike for one hour and 15 minutes.

The man had just pitched a no-hitter! Did he race out and do something exciting and different? No. He did not become a champion by chasing after every thought fleeting through his mind.

The gentleman became a champion through his Daily Success Routine!

Create Your Own Daily Success Routine

1. **Recognize What Is Worthy of Your Total Focus Today.** Everyone will have a different focus. Permit others to stay in the center of their focus. *You* must target what you desire. Everything does not have equal value nor deserve equal time.

2. **Pinpoint The Top 3 Distractions That Occur Habitually.** *The Only Reason Men Fail Is Broken Focus.* Satan cannot *destroy* you but he can *distract* you. You can trace any failure to loss of focus. *What* breaks your focus daily off the things you love the most? *Who* can help you protect your focus?

3. **Pray Continuously In The Holy Spirit.** He has an agenda. Doing so will help you discern *His* agenda, not *yours.*

4. **Determine The Core Product of Your Life.** What do you want to do the most? What is the legacy you desire to leave? What are you willing to walk away from to make it happen?

5. **Embrace Flexibility As An Opportunity.** Hillary Rodham Clinton once said, "I have never had a plan yet where *everything* happened as I planned it." You must be prepared for the *unexpected.*

6. **Recognize Those Around You Who Do Not Have A Determined Focus or Goal.** They want your attention and will not hesitate to unwittingly break your focus.

7. **Discern Those Who Are Oblivious And Blind Toward Your Focus.** I have been dictating books when "friends" would burst into the room distracting me with trivia. *Confront* rudeness.

8. **Keep A Visual Picture of Your Desired Goal And Dream Before You.** Gym walls hold

pictures of physical champions who have won Mr. USA, Miss America, etc., upon them for personal motivation.

Abraham had a picture of the *stars*...the *sand* of the sea as a reminder of God's promise to him of his generations of *children.*

Joseph had a picture of himself in *authority.*

Jesus had a picture of *returning* to the Father.

Become Militant About Keeping Your Daily Success Routine.

What You Keep Doing Daily Is Creating The Future You Have Always Wanted or The Future You Dread.

The Uncommon Woman Develops Her Daily Success Routine.

RECOMMENDED INVESTMENTS:
Seeds of Wisdom on Habits, Vol. 6 (Book/B-18/32 pg)
Seeds of Wisdom on Motivating Yourself, Vol. 31 (Book/B-171/32 pg)
You Will Love Our Website..! WisdomOnline.com

The Proof of Humility
Is The Willingness
To Reach.

-MIKE MURDOCK

Copyright © 2010 by Mike Murdock • Wisdom International
The Wisdom Center • 4051 Denton Hwy. • Ft. Worth, TX 76117

～ 29 ～

THE UNCOMMON WOMAN CONTINUALLY REACHES FOR GREATNESS

Habits Create Greatness.

The Uncommon Woman Pursues Greatness. One of the happiest seasons of my life was years ago when I birthed My Personal Daily Success Routine:

I went to bed at 10:30 p.m. with a cup of hot chocolate. I arose at 5:30 a.m. and walked 3 miles. I repeated this 3 mile walk each night.

My *joy* was remarkable.

My *peace* was unexplainable.

After several weeks, a friend rushed into my hotel room wanting my help on a special letter to his congregation and partners.

Desiring to maintain my momentum, I told him about my Daily Success Routine. It was late and I needed to sleep. He laughed it off, kept talking and finally left at 1:00 a.m.

My *entire rhythm* was deeply affected.

I was unable to arise at 5:30 the next morning and pray, so I decided I would pray at 8:00 a.m.

Every appointment the next day had to be *changed.* Something was lost that I cannot explain. I was unable to *recapture* the *rhythm* of that habit for many months.

A good habit is too powerful to treat lightly. Become militant about keeping it.

What You Look At The Longest Will Become The Strongest.

It will require *total focus* to create Your Daily Success Routine. When you change your daily routine, you will unlock the Promised Harvest for your family, and the work of God.

7 Daily Habits In The Life of The Uncommon Woman

1. The Uncommon Woman Arises At The Same Time Every Morning. John R. Rice, the famous Baptist evangelist of many years ago, would often arrive home from his crusades at 3:00 a.m. or 4:00 a.m. on Monday. But his staff declared, "Regardless of when he arrived, he was at the office the same time each morning!"

2. The Uncommon Woman Starts Her Work At The Same Time Each Day. One of my close friends told me, "The wealthiest man in our town backs out of his driveway at 7:55 every morning...without fail. Mike, I can set my clock by it."

He has a Daily Success Routine.

Ernest Hemingway, the famed writer, wrote every night from 12 a.m. until 6:00 a.m. and then he would sleep from 6:00 a.m. to 2:00 p.m.

Many prolific writers in America have a *Daily Success Routine,* writing the same hours every day.

3. The Uncommon Woman Is Disciplined To Pray At The Same Time Every Day. David did. "Early will I seek Thee." Daniel prayed 3 times a day.

Always establish a consistent appointment in The Secret Place. Doing this will radically change your life. It may be for 5 minutes, but do it daily. Make it a part of your Daily Success Routine.

4.   The Uncommon Woman Reads The Word of God Daily As A Part of Her Success Routine. Reading 3 chapters a day (and 5 on Sundays) will enable you to complete the Bible once a year.

Do not wait until you "have time." If you do, you will never find time for Bible reading.

Your success routine in The Word will *saturate* your spirit with the thoughts and presence of God. Nothing is more important than your appointment in The Secret Place each day reading The Word of God.

His Word will *wash* your mind, *stimulate* your faith and put a *picture* of your Best Friend before you, The Holy Spirit.

5.   The Uncommon Woman   Habitually Speaks   Words   of   Hope,   Confidence   And Expectation of Excellence. Words create your Future. Your *words* of faith and enthusiasm are the *fuel* that unleashes the promised Harvest produced by your Daily Success Routine.

6.   The Uncommon Woman Has A Habit of Planning Her Day. The late Mary Kay Ash, the famed multimillionaire, planned every day with a simple list of 6 things to do.

Mark McCormack, owner of the sports agency IMG, invests one hour every morning in planning the next 23 hours. He plans his day for one solid hour before doing anything else.

7.   The Uncommon Woman Exercises Every Day of Her Life. President Harry Truman walked an hour every day until he was almost 80 years of age. Mr.

Truman had determined the Daily Success Routine that helped create his Future.

Concluding Chapter Thoughts

Protect the Gift of Passion within you.

Guard your Focus every hour.

Be ruthless with distractions.

Feed the picture of your Goals continually.

You may start small or with very little. But when what you love begins to consume your Mind, your Thoughts, Conversation and Schedule...you will experience extraordinary success.

The Uncommon Woman Continually Reaches For Greatness.

RECOMMENDED INVESTMENTS:
Seeds of Wisdom on Habits (Book/B-18/32 pg)
1 Minute Pocket Bible For Women (Book/B-61/134 pg)
The Mentor's Manna On The Secret Place (Book/B-78/32 pg)
The Greatest Success Habit On Earth (Book/B-80/32 pg)
You Will Love Our Website..! WisdomOnline.com

❧ 30 ❧

THE UNCOMMON WOMAN WILL ENCOUNTER 3 TYPES OF PEOPLE

Your Future Holds Great Expectations.

In order to reach your expected end you will have to deal effectively with 3 types of people.

These types of folks are what I describe as *Yesterday, Today* and *Tomorrow* people.

Those that God used Yesterday may not have a place in your Future.

Do not be troubled by this. Instead, move quickly toward the promises of God and prepare to enter your Future *without* Yesterday people.

You do not have to repeat the same mistakes of Yesterday. You have more knowledge today than you have ever had in your entire lifetime.

You have learned from the *pain.*

You have learned from your *losses.*

You have watched carefully and documented what has happened in the lives of others. Do not fear that Yesterday will crawl behind you like a predator and choke you to death.

Continuously Look For The New. "Remember ye not the former things, neither consider the things of old. Behold, I will do a new thing; now it shall spring forth;

shall ye not know it? I will even make a way in the wilderness, and rivers in the desert," (Isaiah 43:18-19).

Focus On Tomorrow. "Forgetting those things which are behind, and reaching forth unto those things which are before, I press toward the mark for the prize of the high calling of God in Christ Jesus," (Philippians 3:13-14).

Know That Intolerance of Your Present Schedules Your Future. As long as you can adapt to the Present... you really do not have a Future.

I am fascinated that Ruth was willing to leave everything comfortable to pursue her Future.

She *refused* to let her religious background become the noose around her neck that would have *sabotaged* her Future.

Ruth *refused* to let her Past rob her of the *potential* of *Tomorrow.* (See Ruth 1:16-18.) She consistently *refused* to build her Future around her *Past.*

Some of us continue to engage in *mental replays* of painful experiences from Yesterday. Some have built our entire lifestyle around one catastrophic experience.

Conversations are even consumed with negative occurrences of 10 years ago. This is dangerous and devastating.

Words Impart Life.

When you discuss your Past, you *perpetuate* Past experiences. If you *repeatedly* replay painful confrontations and situations, you are giving them life and a Future.

When You Replay The Past, You Poison The Present.

The Uncommon Woman Will Encounter 3 Types of People.

❦ 31 ❦

THE UNCOMMON WOMAN IS AWARE HER STRENGTH COMES FROM THE HOLY SPIRIT

━━━━━▶◦◦◦◀━━━━━

The Holy Spirit Is A Person.

He is totally and completely...God. The Holy Spirit has eternally existed alongside God The Father and Jesus The Son. Sadly, much of Christianity knows very little about The Holy Spirit. Some know the symbolic things used to describe Him.

He does move as freely as the *wind.*

But, He is *not* wind.

He is as graceful and gentle as a *dove.*

But, He is *not* a dove.

He cleanses and purifies like *fire.*

But, He is *not* fire.

He is all powerful.

He is both a Gift and a Giver of Gifts.

He is the One Who reveals Jesus.

He is the One Who baptizes believers into their salvation experience with Jesus Christ.

4 Things The Holy Spirit Is To Believers

1.   **The Holy Spirit Is Your Enabler.** "But ye shall receive power, after that the Holy Ghost is come upon you," (Acts 1:8).

2.   **The Holy Spirit Is Your Comforter.** "But when the Comforter is come, Whom I will send unto you from the Father, even the Spirit of truth, which proceedeth from the Father, He shall testify of Me," (John 15:26).

3.   **The Holy Spirit Is Your Teacher.** "He shall teach you all things, and bring all things to your remembrance, whatsoever I have said unto you," (John 14:26).

4.   **The Holy Spirit Is The Revealer of Those Things, Which Are To Come.** "Howbeit when He, the Spirit of truth, is come, He will guide you into all truth," (John 16:13).

Become acquainted with The Holy Spirit. As you come to know Him, truth will explode within your innermost being changing everything around you.

As you become better acquainted with The Holy Spirit you will realize:

Your *best* days are ahead of you.

Your *worst* days are behind you.

Life has a way of bogging us down.

Your relationship with The Holy Spirit will *enable* you to focus your *energy* on our Future.

The Uncommon Woman Is Aware Her Strength Comes From The Holy Spirit.

DECISION

Will You Accept Jesus As Your Personal Savior Today?

The Bible says, "That if thou shalt confess with thy mouth the Lord Jesus, and shalt believe in thine heart that God hath raised Him from the dead, thou shalt be saved," (Romans 10:9).

Pray this prayer from your heart today!

"Dear Jesus, I believe that You died for me and rose again on the third day. I confess I am a sinner...I need Your love and forgiveness...Come into my heart. Forgive my sins. I receive Your eternal life. Confirm Your love by giving me peace, joy and supernatural love for others. Amen."

CLIP AND MAIL

DR. MIKE MURDOCK

is in tremendous demand as one of the most dynamic speakers in America today.

More than 17,000 audiences in over 100 countries have attended his Schools of Wisdom and conferences. Hundreds of invitations come to him from churches, colleges and business corporations. He is a noted author of over 250 books, including the best sellers, *The Leadership Secrets of Jesus* and *Secrets of the Richest Man Who Ever Lived.* Thousands view his weekly television program, *Wisdom Keys with Mike Murdock.* Many attend his Schools of Wisdom that he hosts in many cities of America.

☐ Yes, Mike! I made a decision to accept Christ as my personal Savior today. Please send me my free gift of your book, *31 Keys to a New Beginning* to help me with my new life in Christ.

NAME _____ BIRTHDAY _____

ADDRESS _____

CITY _____ STATE ZIP _____

PHONE _____ EMAIL _____

Mail to: **The Wisdom Center** · 4051 Denton Hwy. · Ft. Worth, TX 76117
1-817-759-BOOK · 1-817-759-2665 · 1-817-759-0300
You Will Love Our Website..! WisdomOnline.com

DR. MIKE MURDOCK

1 Has embraced his Assignment to Pursue...Proclaim...and Publish the Wisdom of God to help people achieve their dreams and goals.

2 Preached his first public sermon at the age of 8.

3 Preached his first evangelistic crusade at the age of 15.

4 Began full-time evangelism at the age of 19, which has continued since 1966.

5 Has traveled and spoken to more than 17,000 audiences in over 100 countries, including East and West Africa, Asia, Europe and South America.

6 Noted author of over 250 books, including best sellers, *Wisdom for Winning, Dream Seeds, The Double Diamond Principle, The Law of Recognition* and *The Holy Spirit Handbook.*

7 Created the popular *Topical Bible* series for Businessmen, Mothers, Fathers, Teenagers; *The One-Minute Pocket Bible* series, and *The Uncommon Life* series.

8 The Creator of The Master 7 Mentorship System, an Achievement Program for Believers.

9 Has composed thousands of songs such as "I Am Blessed," "You Can Make It," "God Rides On Wings of Love" and "Jesus, Just The Mention of Your Name," recorded by many gospel artists.

10 Is the Founder and Senior Pastor of The Wisdom Center, in Fort Worth, Texas...a Church with International Ministry around the world.

11 Host of *Wisdom Keys with Mike Murdock,* a weekly TV Program seen internationally.

12 Has appeared often on TBN, CBN, BET, Daystar, Inspirational Network, LeSea Broadcasting and other television network programs.

13 Has led over 3,000 to accept the call into full-time ministry.

THE MINISTRY

1 **Wisdom Books & Literature** - Over 250 best-selling Wisdom Books and 70 Teaching Tape Series.

2 **Church Crusades** - Multitudes are ministered to in crusades and seminars throughout America in "The Uncommon Wisdom Conferences." Known as a man who loves pastors, he has focused on church crusades for over 43 years.

3 **Music Ministry** - Millions have been blessed by the anointed songwriting and singing of Mike Murdock, who has made over 15 music albums and CDs available.

4 **Television** - *Wisdom Keys with Mike Murdock,* a nationally-syndicated weekly television program.

5 **The Wisdom Center** - The Church and Ministry Offices where Dr. Murdock speaks weekly on Wisdom for The Uncommon Life.

6 **Schools of The Holy Spirit** - Mike Murdock hosts Schools of The Holy Spirit in many churches to mentor believers on the Person and Companionship of The Holy Spirit.

7 **Schools of Wisdom** - In many major cities Mike Murdock hosts Schools of Wisdom for those who want personalized and advanced training for achieving "The Uncommon Dream."

8 **Missions Outreach** - Dr. Mike Murdock's overseas outreaches to over 100 countries have included crusades in East and West Africa, Asia, Europe and South America.

Are You Watching My Daily TV Program..?

Dr. Mike Murdock

PST
7:30p
Wed
Daystar

8:30p
Mon-Fri
WORD

8:30p
Wed
INSP

MST
8:30p
Wed
Daystar

9:30p
Mon-Fri
WORD

9:30p
Wed
INSP

CST
9:30p
Wed
Daystar

10:30p
Mon-Fri
WORD

10:30p
Wed
INSP

EST
10:30p
Wed
Daystar

11:30p
Mon-Fri
WORD

11:30p
Wed
INSP

Check Your Local Listings... For Channels And Schedules

Visit Our Website Today..! WisdomOnline.com

PODCAST..!
2 MINUTE WISDOM WITH DR. MIKE MURDOCK..!
(Audio/Video Teachings)

Stay Connected Anytime... Anywhere.
The Options Are Endless...
Play on your iPod, Mac or PC.

Dr. Mike Murdock

Visit My Website:
WisdomOnline.com
Every Sunday..!
At 10:00a CST

The Wisdom Center Network

Watch The Services From Your Personal Computer...

Simply Go To Our Website:
WisdomOnline.com
Log On To The
Actual 24 Hour-A-Day
Programming!

FREE Downloads!
2 Minute Wisdom, Volume 1
Memory Bible On Miracles
He's A Healing Jesus, Song
48 Miracles Of Jesus

You Will Love Our Website... Visit Today..! WisdomOnline.com

JOIN THE

Wisdom Key 3000

TODAY!

Will You Become My Ministry Partner In The Work of God?

Dear Friend,

God has connected us!

I have asked The Holy Spirit for 3000 Special Partners who will plant a monthly Seed of $58.00 to help me bring the gospel around the world. (58 represents 58 kinds of blessings in the Bible.)

Will you become my monthly Faith Partner in The Wisdom Key 3000? Your monthly Seed of $58.00 is so powerful in helping heal broken lives. When you sow into the work of God, 4 Miracle Harvests are guaranteed in Scripture, Isaiah 58...

- ▸ Uncommon Health (Isaiah 58)
- ▸ Uncommon Wisdom For Decision-Making (Isaiah 58)
- ▸ Uncommon Financial Favor (Isaiah 58)
- ▸ Uncommon Family Restoration (Isaiah 58)

Your Faith Partner,

Mike Murdock

P.S. Please clip the coupon attached and return it to me today, so I can rush the Wisdom Key Partnership Pak to you... or call me at 1-817-759-0300.

☐ *Yes Mike, I want to join The Wisdom Key 3000.*
    Please rush The Wisdom Key Partnership Pak to me today!
☐ *Enclosed is my first monthly Seed-Faith Promise of:*
        ☐ *$58* ☐ *Other $_____.*

☐CHECK ☐MONEY ORDER ☐AMEX ☐DISCOVER ☐MASTERCARD ☐VISA

edit Card # _____ Exp. ____/____

gnature _____

ame _____ Birth Date ____/____

dress _____

ty _____ State _____ Zip _____

one _____ EMail _____

r Seed-Faith Offerings are used to support The Wisdom Center, and all of its programs. The Wisdom Center reserves the right to
rect funds as needed in order to carry out our charitable purpose. In the event The Wisdom Center receives more funds for the
ect than needed, the excess will be used for another worthy outreach. (Your transactions may be electronically deposited.)

WK304

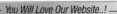

THE WISDOM CENTER
4051 Denton Highway • Fort Worth, TX 76117

1-817-759-BOOK
1-817-759-2665
1-817-759-0300

— *You Will Love Our Website..!* —
WisdomOnline.com

It Could Happen

$1,000 Gift Received..!

The first time I saw you, you asked for an offering of $58 and said that in 58 days we would receive a blessing. On exactly the 58th day, I received a $1,000 check from one of my real estate clients as a gift. I had given her advice on refinancing, but wasn't expecting anything back. God bless you!

F. B. - Philadelphia, PA

Exchange of Business Services And...A Car..!

I made a $58 pledge to your ministry. The following day, I went to the dentist to have $600 of dental work done. The dentist's office had flooded and was in need of cleaning. So, I offered the services of my cleaning business so I could pay my bill. They gave me the job in exchange for the entire dental bill! But that isn't all!!! You said to write on the Seed check what we were believing for. I had written "a car". Just days later, I got my car...a Nissan Altima and IT IS PAID FOR!!

D. A. - Denham Springs, LA

Increase In Salary..!

My wife and I sowed into your ministry believing for financial blessings this year. I want to report that I have just started a new position as marketing strategist with a major midwest law firm and received a salary increase of nearly $10,000. Thank you incredibly... your prayers and words of Wisdom are precious to us.

R. D. - Depauw, IN

To You!

Debt Cancellation..!

I sent a $58 Seed…believing God to cancel my son's debt. He had brain surgery; but he did not have any insurance. The surgery cost around $17,000. But the doctor said he would waive the debt!

N. B. - McMinnville, TN

Job Offer..!

I was moved to assist your ministry with $58 per month partnership. When I saw you on television, I gave immediately. I had been praying for a job. That night, as I was picking up my husband from work, one of the physicians was coming out and he offered me a job! Your ministry is fertile soil to sow my Seed.

K. L. - Las Pinas City, Philippines

Salvation of A Loved One..!

Dr. Murdock told me that my $58 Seed was going to cause a loved one to get saved. After 23 years of my daughter being backslid, she came back to God…

L. B. - East Saint Louis, IL

Salary Doubled..!

…you said to sow a $1,000 Seed and expect a miracle within 90 days. Within 60 days of sowing it, I was offered a very unexpected job. Less than 30 days after that, I had relocated…to start my new job, which pays double my previous salary.

M. H. - Arlington, TX

WisdomOnline.com

DR. MIKE MURDOCK

Click!

**Visit Today!
Updated Daily..!**

- Bookstore
- Current Events
- Daily Wisdom Keys
- Free Downloads!
- Free Wisdom Key
  Screen Savers
- Free Subscription To
  Wisdom Digest
- Find Great Gift Ideas
- Itinerary of
  DR. MIKE MURDOCK
- Media Center
  CD/DVD/Tapes
- Ministry Outreach

- Partner Care Center
- Projects-in-Progress
- Shop Online
- Streaming LIVE!
- Upcoming Events
- Video-of-The-Day
- Wisdom-Talk-of-The-Day...
  Every Day...!
- Wisdom Times
- Wisdom Product Paks
- *And Much More!*

FREE *Books*

FREE *Downloads*

FREE *Music*

Click On The 🔢 Free Downloads! Button...

You Will Love Our Website..! WisdomOnline.com

Miracle 7 BOOK PAK!

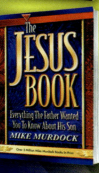

DR. MIKE MURDOCK

❶ **Dream Seeds** (Book/B-11/106pg/$9)

❷ **7 Hidden Keys to Favor** (Book/B-119/32pg/$7)

❸ **Seeds of Wisdom on Miracles** (Book/B-15/32pg/$3)

❹ **Seeds of Wisdom on Prayer** (Book/B-23/32pg/$3)

❺ **The Jesus Book** (Book/B-27/166pg/$10)

❻ **The Memory Bible on Miracles** (Book/B-208/32pg/$3)

❼ **The Mentor's Manna on Attitude** (Book/B-58/32pg/$3)

The Wisdom Center
Miracle 7 Book Pak!
Only $**30** $36 Value
WBL-24
Wisdom Is The Principal Thing

Add 20% For S/H

Quantity Prices Available Upon Request

Each Wisdom Book may be purchased separately if so desired.

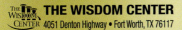

THE WISDOM CENTER
4051 Denton Highway • Fort Worth, TX 76117

1-817-759-BOOK
1-817-759-2665
1-817-759-0300

You Will Love Our Website..!
WISDOMONLINE.COM   A

Crisis 7 BOOK PAK!

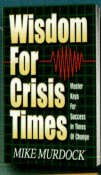
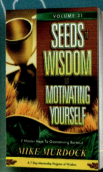

DR. MIKE MURDOCK

❶ **The Survival Bible** (Book/B-29/248pg/$10)

❷ **Wisdom For Crisis Times** (Book/B-40/112pg/$9)

❸ **Seeds of Wisdom on Motivating Yourself** (Book/B-171/32pg/$5)

❹ **Seeds of Wisdom on Overcoming** (Book/B-17/32pg/$3)

❺ **Seeds of Wisdom on Warfare** (Book/B-19/32pg/$5)

❻ **Battle Techniques For War-Weary Saints** (Book/B-07/32pg/$5)

❼ **Seeds of Wisdom on Adversity** (Book/B-21/32pg/$3)

The Wisdom Center
Crisis 7 Book Pak!
Only $**30** $40 Value

WBL-25

Wisdom Is The Principal Thing

Add 20% For S/H

Quantity Prices Available Upon Request

Each Wisdom Book may be purchased separately if so desired.

B THE WISDOM CENTER
4051 Denton Highway • Fort Worth, TX 76117

1-817-759-BOOK
1-817-759-2665
1-817-759-0300

You Will Love Our Website..!
WISDOMONLINE.COM

Money 7 BOOK PAK!

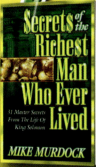

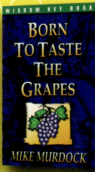

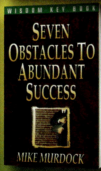
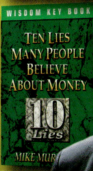

DR. MIKE MURDOCK

❶ **Secrets of the Richest Man Who Ever Lived** (Book/B-99/179pg/$10)

❷ **The Blessing Bible** (Book/B-28/252pg/$10)

❸ **Born To Taste The Grapes** (Book/B-65/32pg/$3)

❹ **Creating Tomorrow Through Seed-Faith** (Book/B-06/32pg/$5)

❺ **Seeds of Wisdom on Prosperity** (Book/B-22/32pg/$5)

❻ **Seven Obstacles To Abundant Success** (Book/B-64/32pg/$5)

❼ **Ten Lies Many People Believe About Money** (Book/B-04/32pg/$5)

The Wisdom Center
Money 7 Book Pak!
Only $**30** $43 Value
WBL-30
Wisdom Is The Principal Thing

Add 20% For S/H

Each Wisdom Book may be purchased separately if so desired.

THE WISDOM CENTER
4051 Denton Highway • Fort Worth, TX 76117

1-817-759-**BOOK**
1-817-759-**2665**
1-817-759-**0300**

You Will Love Our Website..!
WISDOMONLINE.COM

C

Career 7

Book Pak For Business People!

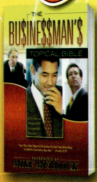

DR. MIKE MURDOCK

❶ The Businessman's Topical Bible (Book/B-33/384pg/$10)

❷ 31 Secrets for Career Success (Book/B-44/112pg/$10)

❸ 31 Scriptures Every Businessman Should Memorize (Book/B-141/32pg/$3)

❹ 7 Overlooked Keys To Effective Goal-Setting (Book/B-127/32pg/$7)

❺ 7 Rewards of Problem Solving (Book/B-118/32pg/$7)

❻ How To Double Your Productivity In 24 Hours (Book/B-137/32pg/$7)

❼ The Mentor's Manna on Achievement (Book/B-79/32pg/$5)

Each Wisdom Book may be purchased separately if so desired.

The Wisdom Center
Career 7 Book Pak!
Only $**30** $49 Value
WBL-27
Wisdom Is The Principal Thing

Add 20% S&H

D **THE WISDOM CENTER**
4051 Denton Highway • Fort Worth, TX 76117

1-817-759-BOOK
1-817-759-2665
1-817-759-0300

You Will Love Our Website..!
WISDOMONLINE.COM

Unforgettable Woman 4
Book Pak!

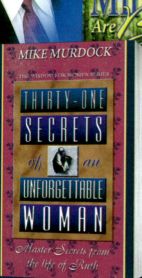
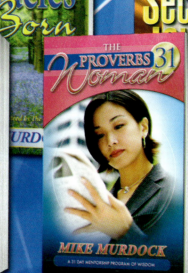

1 **Where Miracles Are Born** (Book/B-115/32pg/$7)

2 **Secrets of The Journey, Vol. 6** (Book/B-102/32pg/$5)

3 **Thirty-One Secrets of an Unforgettable Woman** (Book/B-57/140pg/$12)

4 **The Proverbs 31 Woman** (Book/B-49/70pg/$7)

Each Wisdom Book may be purchased separately if so desired.

The Wisdom Center
Unforgettable Woman 4 Book Pak!
Only **$20** $31 Value
PAK-31
Wisdom Is The Principal Thing

Add 20% For S/H

THE WISDOM CENTER
4051 Denton Highway · Fort Worth, TX 76117

1-817-759-BOOK
1-817-759-2665
1-817-759-0300

You Will Love Our Website..!
WISDOMONLINE.COM

E

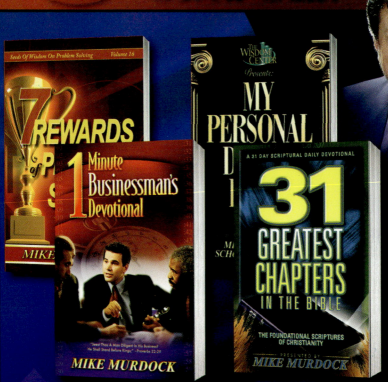

The Businessman's Devotional 4 Book Pak!

1 7 Rewards of Problem Solving (Book/B-118/32pg/$7)

2 My Personal Dream Book (Book/B-143/32pg/$7)

3 1 Minute Businessman's Devotional
(Book/B-42/224pg/$12)

4 31 Greatest Chapters In The Bible
(Book/B-54/138pg/$10)

The Wisdom Center
The Businessman's Devotional 4 Book Pak!
Only $20 $36 Value
PAK-22
Wisdom Is The Principal Thing

Add 20% For S/H

F THE WISDOM CENTER 4051 Denton Highway • Fort Worth, TX 76117

1-817-759-BOOK
1-817-759-2665
1-817-759-0300

You Will Love Our Website..!
WISDOMONLINE.COM

Millionaire-Talk

SCHOOL of FINANCIAL SUCCESS SERIES

31 THINGS You Will Need To Become A MILLIONAIRE

Your Financial Future Is Determined By The Instruction You Are Willing To Follow.

FREE BOOK ENCLOSED!

Master 7 Mentorship Program *Mike Murdock*

DR. MIKE MURDOCK

MY GIFT OF APPRECIATION
GIFT of Appreciation
Wisdom Is The Principal Thing

31 Things You Will Need To Become A Millionaire (2-CD's/WCPL-116)

Topics Include:

- You Will Need Financial Heroes
- Your Willingness To Negotiate Everything
- You Must Have The Ability To Transfer Your Enthusiasm, Your Vision To Others
- Know Your Competition
- Be Willing To Train Your Team Personally As To Your Expectations
- Hire Professionals To Do A Professional's Job

I have asked the Lord for 3,000 special partners who will sow an extra Seed of $58 towards our Television Outreach Ministry. Your Seed is so appreciated! Remember to request your Gift CD's, 2 Disc Volume, *31 Things You Will Need To Become A Millionaire,* when you write this week!

THE WISDOM CENTER
4051 Denton Highway • Fort Worth, TX 76117

1-817-759-BOOK
1-817-759-2665
1-817-759-0300

You Will Love Our Website..!
WISDOMONLINE.COM

G

CHAMPIONS 4
Book Pak!

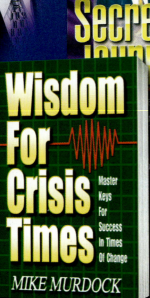

❶ Secrets of The Journey, Vol. 3 (Book/B-94/32pg/$5)

❷ My Personal Dream Book (Book/B-143/32pg/$7)

❸ Wisdom For Crisis Times
(Book/B-40/112pg/$9)

❹ The Making of A Champion
(Book/B-59/128pg/$10)

The Wisdom Center
Champions 4 Book Pak!
Only $20 $31 Value
PAK-23
Wisdom Is The Principal Thing

Each Wisdom Book may be purchased separately if so desired.

Add 20% For S/H

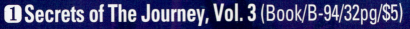

H **THE WISDOM CENTER**
4051 Denton Highway · Fort Worth, TX 76117

1-817-759-BOOK
1-817-759-2665
1-817-759-0300

You Will Love Our Website..!
WISDOMONLINE.COM

Increase 4
Book Pak!

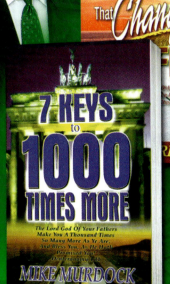

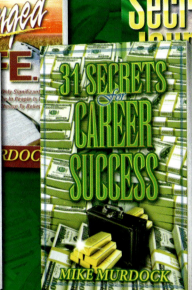

1 The Book That Changed My Life... (Book/B-117/32pg/$7)

2 Secrets of The Journey, Vol. 2 (Book/B-93/32pg/$5)

3 7 Keys to 1000 Times More
(Book/B-104/128pg/$10)

4 31 Secrets for Career Success
(Book/B-44/112pg/$10)

The Wisdom Center
Increase 4 Book Pak!
Only $**20** $32 Value
PAK-26
Wisdom Is The Principal Thing

Each Wisdom Book may be purchased separately if so desired.

Add 20% For S/H

THE WISDOM CENTER
4051 Denton Highway · Fort Worth, TX 76117

1-817-759-BOOK
1-817-759-2665
1-817-759-0300

— You Will Love Our Website..! —
WISDOMONLINE.COM

The Mentorship 7 *Book Pak!*

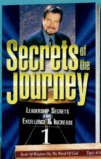
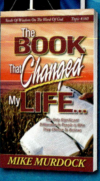

❶ 31 Facts About Wisdom
(Book/B-46/32pg/$5)

❷ Secrets of The Journey, Vol. 1
(Book/B-92/32pg/$5)

❸ 7 Rewards of Problem Solving (Book/B-118/32pg/$7)

❹ My Personal Dream Book
(Book/B-143/32pg/$5)

❺ The Wisdom Key Devotional
(Book/B-165/60pg/$10)

❻ The Book That Changed My Life...
(Book/B-117/32pg/$7)

❼ Where Miracles Are Born
(Book/B-115/32pg/$7)

All 7 Books For One Great Price!

The Wisdom Center
The Mentorship 7 Book Pak!
Only **$20** $46 Value
PAK-25
Wisdom Is The Principal Thing

Each Wisdom Book may be purchased separately if so desired.

Add 20% For S/H

J   THE WISDOM CENTER
4051 Denton Highway · Fort Worth, TX 76117

1-817-759-BOOK
1-817-759-2665
1-817-759-0300

— *You Will Love Our Website..!*
WISDOMONLINE.COM

35 Success-Notes..!

That Can Unlock Your Dreams And Goals!

Order Your FREE Personal Copy Today!

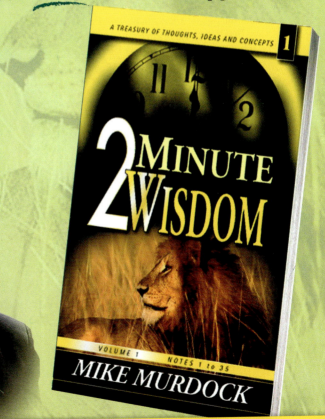

A TREASURY OF THOUGHTS, IDEAS AND CONCEPTS · 1

2 MINUTE WISDOM

VOLUME 1 · NOTES 1 to 35

MIKE MURDOCK

Download It For Free On WisdomOnline.com

THE WISDOM CENTER
4051 Denton Highway · Fort Worth, TX 76117

1-817-759-BOOK
1-817-759-2665
1-817-759-0300

You Will Love Our Website..!
WISDOMONLINE.COM

K

THE WISDOM BIBLE

Partnership Edition

Over 120 Wisdom Study Guides Included Such As:

- ▶ 10 Qualities of Uncommon Achievers
- ▶ 18 Facts You Should Know About The Anointing
- ▶ 21 Facts To Help You Identify Those Assigned To You
- ▶ 31 Facts You Should Know About Your Assignment
- ▶ 8 Keys That Unlock Victory In Every Attack
- ▶ 22 Defense Techniques To Remember During Seasons of Personal Attack
- ▶ 20 Wisdom Keys And Techniques To Remember During An Uncommon Battle
- ▶ 11 Benefits You Can Expect From God
- ▶ 31 Facts You Should Know About Favor
- ▶ The Covenant of 58 Blessings
- ▶ 7 Keys To Receiving Your Miracle
- ▶ 16 Facts You Should Remember About Contentious People
- ▶ 5 Facts Solomon Taught About Contracts
- ▶ 7 Facts You Should Know About Conflict
- ▶ 6 Steps That Can Unlock Your Self-Confidence
- ▶ And Much More!

Your Partnership makes such a difference in The Wisdom Center Outreach Ministries. I wanted to place a Gift in your hand that could last a lifetime for you and your family...**The Wisdom Study Bible.**

40 Years of Personal Notes...this Partnership Edition Bible contains 160 pages of my Personal Study Notes...that could forever change your Bible Study of The Word of God. This **Partnership Edition...**is my personal **Gift of Appreciation** when you sow your Sponsorship Seed of $1,000 to help us complete The Prayer Center and TV Studio Complex. An Uncommon Seed Always Creates An Uncommon Harvest!

Mike

Thank you from my heart for your Seed of Obedience (Luke 6:38).

THE WISDOM CENTER 4051 Denton Highway • Fort Worth, TX 76117

1-817-759-BOOK
1-817-759-2665
1-817-759-0300

You Will Love Our Website..!
WISDOMONLINE.COM

L

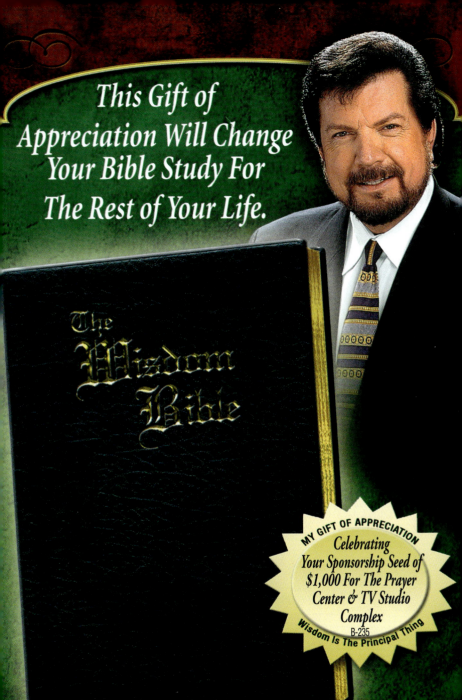

This Gift of
Appreciation Will Change
Your Bible Study For
The Rest of Your Life.

The Wisdom Bible

MY GIFT OF APPRECIATION
Celebrating
Your Sponsorship Seed of
$1,000 For The Prayer
Center & TV Studio
Complex
B-235
Wisdom Is The Principal Thing

THE WISDOM CENTER
4051 Denton Highway • Fort Worth, TX 76117
1-817-759-BOOK
1-817-759-2665
1-817-759-0300
You Will Love Our Website..!
WISDOMONLINE.COM   M

7 Hidden Ingredients In Every Miracle...

The Hidden Secrets That Cause Miracles To Happen.

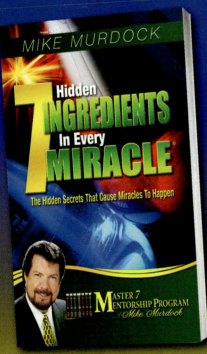

You Will Learn:

- ▶ How To Apply The Scriptural Formula In Every Prayer
- ▶ 3 Ways To Build Your Faith To Mountain-Moving Level
- ▶ Why Some Miracles Are Delayed Unnecessarily
- ▶ The Hidden Prescription For Silencing Demonic Voices In Your Environment

The Wisdom Center

ONLY $7

B-280

Wisdom Is The Principal Thing

AMERICAN EXPRESS DISCOVER MasterCard VISA

Add 20% For S/H

N

THE WISDOM CENTER
4051 Denton Highway · Fort Worth, TX 76117

1-817-759-BOOK
1-817-759-2665
1-817-759-0300

— You Will Love Our Website..! —
WISDOMONLINE.COM